WHISTLEBERRIES, STIRABOUT, & DEPRESSION CAKE

WHISTLEBERRIES, STIRABOUT, & DEPRESSION CAKE

Edward B. Reynolds

Michael Kennedy

FEDERAL WRITERS' PROJECT

Foreword by Greg Patent

A ThreeForks™ Book

ThreeForks is an imprint of Falcon Publishing

A ThreeForks Book

ThreeForks is an imprint of Falcon® Publishing, Inc.

© 2000 Falcon® Publishing, Inc., Helena, Montana
Printed in Canada.

1 2 3 4 5 6 7 8 9 0 TP 05 04 03 02 01 00

All photos from the WPA collection, Merrill G. Burlingame Special Collections in the Renne Library at Montana State University, Bozeman.
Cover photos are details of photos appearing on pages vi and 70. All photo credits appear on page 89.
Cover design, book design, and page composition by Jeff Wincapaw.

Cataloging-in-Publication Data is on file at the Library of Congress.

For extra copies of this book and information about other ThreeForks books, write Falcon, P.O. Box 1718, Helena, Montana 59624; or call 1-800-582-2665. You can also visit our website at www.Falcon.com or contact us by e-mail at falcon@falcon.com.

A portion of the proceeds from the sale of this book will be donated for library development at Montana State University, Bozeman.

Contents

Foreword

by Greg Patent

"TWO YOUNG COWBOYS WHO RODE THE RANGE TOGETHER, BOTH BEING VERY HEARTY, WHEN AT THE RANCH OR ROUND-UP WAGON THEY WOULD GO TO THE CUPBOARD AND LUNCH ON ANY LEFT-OVERS THEY WERE ABLE TO FIND. A NEW COOK WAS HIRED AT THE RANCH WHERE THEY WERE WORKING. The first night after the new cook's arrival they waited until the cook had gone to bed before raiding the lunch cupboard, it being dark and them being afraid of waking the cook, who had made changes in the cupboard during the first day. At last they found the sugar bowl and cream pitcher, then something in a nice clean jar. They poured the sugar and cream into the jar stirring it well, being as quiet as possible to avoid waking the cook whose room was near the kitchen. One was heard to ask the other in a whisper what it was. He remarked, 'I don't know what it is, but it's laurpin good truck.' Meaning very good. The next morning the cook had to make baking powder biscuits as these boys had eaten up the sour dough, making it good to eat by adding the cream and sugar. These special dishes are often called laurpin good truck when asked for during the meal."

Source: Oscar L. Canoy, Miles City Montana, November 17 to 28, 1941. Found in the correspondence in the Montana WPA collection (Box 2, File 3).

This vivid story may never have been documented without the existence of the Federal Writers' Project division of the depression era's Works

Projects Administration. Between 1935 and 1942, as part of its effort to
create employment for everyone, the U.S. government posted job offerings
for writers, journalists, editors, researchers, geologists, map draftsmen, and
other professionals to prepare material for the American Guide Books by
collecting information ranging from an area's local history to its scenery. The
overall aim was to research whatever made up the life of communities in the
United States. The Montana Writers' Project collection alone included more
than 250,000 items and occupied 57 linear feet of storage space. Since food
and the social customs associated with it play such crucial roles in our lives,
one of the major goals of the Federal Writers' Project was to publish a mon-
umental book, "America Eats," detailing group eating as an important
American social institution. Describing American food customs in the five
regions of the United States—the Northeast, South, Midwest, Far West, and
Southwest—became the objective, and a daunting one at that. To that end,
writing teams set out to investigate social customs and attitudes toward food
throughout the forty-eight states.

Unfortunately, the entrance of the United States into World War II
forced the discontinuation of the Writers' Project. By then, however,
Michael Kennedy, Supervisor of the Montana State Writers' Project, and
Edward B. Reynolds, Editor, had already sifted through and organized the
findings of their Far West group and written a manuscript for the regional
section of the national project. The complete volume, "America Eats," never
materialized, and this Far West portion of the historical treasure languished
in the archives for almost sixty years. In 1995 the Montana Cultural Trust
provided funds to help put the material, housed in Special Collections at
Montana State University in Bozeman, Montana, in order. Twenty-five series
documenting different aspects of American culture, including "America
Eats: Far West" came to light.

That the Federal Writers' Project recognized American cookery to be a unique and authentic art worth preserving is laudatory. The government feared that many of our food customs, if not recorded, would soon be lost, because mechanized mass production of foodstuffs was already firmly in place by the 1930s and cooks were already spending less time preparing food from scratch. In 1930 the first prepared biscuit mixes went on sale. Canned goods, factory-baked bread, and frozen foods became commonplace at home meals. Cake mixes, frozen dinners, bottled salad dressings, and other processed foods followed. No wonder the government became concerned about the demise of our cooking heritage.

★   ★   ★

The most awesome feature of the Far West is the vastness of the land and its openness. The nine western states covered in this book occupy almost one-third of the area of the contiguous forty-eight states. This rugged territory stretches from Wyoming's sagebrush plains to the crashing waves battering the salty shores of California, Oregon, and Washington. In between lie the parched Nevada and Utah deserts and the raging rivers and craggy mountains of Colorado, Idaho, and Montana. "Here you will find no lacy frills to catch the eye, or subtle nuances of taste and smell to goad the appetite of the jaded and world-weary gastronome." These words from the opening paragraphs of the text ring as true now as they did more than six decades ago. In many parts of the West, even today, food is basic and of the stick-to-the-ribs variety.

Settled by trappers and fur traders, miners, cattle ranchers, timbermen, and farmers, the rugged western frontier dictated the robust nature of its favorite foods: steaks, roasts, or stews of beef, mutton, and pork; game of all kinds; mountain trout; hearty breakfasts of ham, eggs, and biscuits with gravy; sourdough breads and pancakes. And if you lived along the coast, you feasted on salmon, halibut, and other succulent fish and seafoods. Vigorous hard-working people wanted and needed foods that satisfied their amazing appetites. If gourmets lived to eat, the westerner ate to live.

One joy of this book is learning the colorful language invented to describe certain foods and drink: boxty, cackleberries, whistleberries, whiskey and ditch, Sean O'Farrell, death ball, and grunt are a few examples. I leave the happy discovery of their meanings to you. Smiles and chuckles will surely follow when you read the stories of William Shakespeare's picture hanging in Leadville, Colorado's, Tabor Opera House; the lavish meals served at banquets hosted by the Copper Kings; and the extravagance of gold miners who suddenly struck it rich.

On the range during a cattle drive, the chuck wagon and its cook became the center of life at mealtime. There wasn't much time to eat, since the cowboys had to wolf down their food and leap back on their horses as quickly as possible. Tony Grace, a former chuck wagon cook who worked in seven western states, was 103 years old when I interviewed him several years ago. His recollections of what it was like to prepare breakfast, lunch, and dinner for hungry cowboys during a roundup matches the detailed descriptions in this book, right down to the cooking of Son-of-a-bitch stew, and Son-of-a-gun in a sack. For a cowboy, eating amounted to piling your tin plate with food, filling your tin cup with good strong coffee, and finding a comfortable spot on the ground to chow down. Not much conversation occurred during these meals, just getting the food into your belly in a hurry and moving on to the work that had to be done.

Sheepherders worked in open country, too, isolated and alone just like a prospector, and partaking of similar foods since there was no refrigeration.

Out on the coast, salmon barbecues, crawfish and oyster feeds, and geoduck hunts were favorite pastimes. The details of all these events are described so precisely in this manuscript that you feel you're an active participant. I could swear I was tasting the food being cooked! Or in the case of oysters eaten raw, savoring their slithery, briny flesh. Today the once frequent salmon barbecues on the Columbia River are but a memory, but our passionate appetites for just about all the other seafood can still be satisfied.

In the Mountain West, however, we still have branding parties featuring mountain oysters dipped in cracker crumbs, fried to a crisp golden brown in bacon grease, and outdoor barbecues with juicy three-inch-thick steaks grilled to rare perfection over hot coals. And although many of the businessmen's clubs and social gatherings described in this book no longer exist, ethnic groups, such as the Sons of Norway, have gatherings where singing and dancing are as important as the lutefisk. And the Greek community in Missoula, Montana, hosts an annual traditional dinner with music and dancing. Red Lodge, Montana, celebrates the mining heritage of our state every August in its Festival of Nations, where national dishes of the Scotch, Irish, Serbs, Croats, Germans, and others can be savored by visitors. Every day for a week or so, the cuisine of a particular country is featured in restaurants. Wandering through town I pop into several places, sampling one dish at each one. Many of the staff dress in the costume of the country, and the whole mood is festive and infectious. The special thing about festivals is that the food itself is a celebration and appreciation of life, and in social settings the joy becomes communal. If you are interested in food festivals in western states, check with the state tourist bureaus or visit the states' websites.

The thirty-six recipes at the back of this book come from eight of the nine Far West states. (For unknown reasons none are from California.) Here you will find McGinties, dried apples cooked in a crust and cut into diamond-shaped bars; Wild Duck baked in clay to a tender succulence; Fish Chowder cooked in a Dutch oven over a bed of coals; and Brown Cake, a bittersweet chocolate and walnut loaf. And let me tell you, it's all laurpin good truck!

Sources:

Algren, Nelson. *America Eats*. Iowa City: University of Iowa Press, 1992.

Camp, Charles. *American Foodways: What, When, Why and How We Eat in America*. Little Rock, Ark.: August House, Inc. Publishers, 1989.

Hooker, Richard. *Food and Drink in America*. Indianapolis/New York: Bobbs-Merrill Company, Inc., 1981.

Weaver, William Woys. *America Eats: Forms of Edible Folk Art*. New York: Harper & Row, Publishers, 1989.

GREG PATENT is a food writer and cookbook author who lives in Missoula, Montana. *New Cooking from the Old West*, a collection of contemporary recipes set within a historical context, was published by Ten Speed Press in 1996. His newest book is *A is for Apple,* co-authored with his wife, Dorothy, and published by Broadway Books (1999). He is currently working on a historical cookbook, *Baking in America*, for Houghton Mifflin. He is also a regular contributor to *Cooking Light* magazine and serves on its editorial board.

Editor's Preface

EDWARD B. REYNOLDS AND MICHAEL KENNEDY WROTE THE TEXT FOR THIS VOLUME WITH THE INTENTION THAT IT WOULD BE A SINGLE SECTION IN A MASSIVE VOLUME ON AMERICA'S EATING AND DRINKING HABITS CALLED "AMERICA EATS," AS ENVISIONED BY THE FEDERAL WRITERS' PROJECT (1935–1942). "AMERICA EATS" WAS NEVER PUBLISHED. The archived correspondence does not explain why or how Edward B. Reynolds of Butte, Montana, was chosen to compile the information gathered by field workers in California, Colorado, Idaho, Montana, Nevada, Oregon, Utah, Washington, and Wyoming for the "Far West" portion of the "America Eats" project. We do know, however, that he had to work only with the information gathered and submitted by each state. Certain states were more active in their field research than others, thus weighting the manuscript's anecdotal and historical coverage of those areas. For the publishing of this volume, I did not alter or add to the text completed during the late 1930s and early 1940s.

Michael Kennedy, supervisor of the Montana Writers' Project, worked with Reynolds to edit this portion of "America Eats." The original directive from the Federal Writers' Project office in Washington, D.C., stated that the tone of the "America Eats" writings should be "light, but not tea shoppe, masculine rather than feminine." To preserve the original writing style and in an effort to maintain the intended character of the "America Eats" project, all organization, language, references, and style remain unchanged from the original archived manuscript. The recipes have not been tested. Obvious typographical errors have been corrected.

Megan Hiller

Introduction

TRAVEL WESTWARD INTO THE SLANTING RAYS OF THE SETTING SUN; CROSS THE ERODED BADLANDS AND SAGEBRUSH PLAINS OF WYOMING, EASTERN MONTANA, IDAHO, OR NEVADA; CLIMB THE LOFTY WHITE-CAPPED MOUNTAINS OF WESTERN MONTANA, UTAH, IDAHO, WASHINGTON, OREGON, OR CALIFORNIA; DROP DOWN INTO THE COLUMBIA RIVER BASIN OR STAND ON THE SALT-SPRAYED SHORES OF THE PUGET SOUND AND PACIFIC OCEAN. Do all these things, because they will give you an appetite for the robust foods of the West—foods to satisfy the hunger of a virile people, adventurous and hardy.

Here you will find no lacy frills to catch the eye, or subtle nuances of taste and smell to goad the appetite of the jaded and world-weary gastronome. Few condiments are used in the mountainous portions of the West, for the greatest sauce of all—hunger—is sufficient. Instead of pastries, whipped or fluffed desserts, and delicate dishes, you will find the big, mealy baked potato, creamy and golden from gobs of rich butter; huge ears of corn on the cob, likewise streaming with butter; great roasts and thick steaks, dappled and encrusted with crisp yellow fat, deeply browned on the outside but rare in the center; mountain trout and seafood, thick pies, homemade jellies, jams, and breads.

In the mining camps of Utah, Nevada, Colorado, Idaho, Montana, and California you will find such substantial foods as hot cakes, ham and eggs, potatoes, beef, mutton, and pork cooked in the many ways native to the Irish,

1

Cornish, Welsh, Slavs, and scores of other nationalities who invaded the mines in their search for a better life. Here the sarma of the Serbians and Croatians will be found alongside of the Cousin Jack pasty, the deep bowls of Italian spaghetti, and the Native American foods of the East, Middle West, and South.

In the cattle country of Wyoming, eastern Montana, Nevada—in fact, the entire West—are golden biscuits, mulligan stews, barbecued beef, venison, elk, mountain goat, and other wild game, as well as sourdough pancakes, pies, and similar food. On the Pacific Coast will be found salmon, clams, shrimp, smelt, crabs, cod, halibut, fruit, peas, and other vegetables.

Drinks range from the wines of the coastal fruit country to the hard liquor of the mountains. Beer is a favorite everywhere.

But throughout the West—Montana, Nevada, Idaho, Utah, Colorado, Washington, Oregon, Wyoming, and California—the eating habits are vigorous, based upon the traditions of a recent frontier past, softened by eastern United States and Old World refinements, tempered by modern dietetics, and blended by the many cosmopolitan influences of the immigrants. But always at the base is the need of a vigorous people to satisfy a robust hunger.

Less than a century ago Joe Meek and his buckskin-clad partners stood around a campfire, their beady eyes eagerly watching a kettle of boiling water. The reflected light of the dancing flames gave a ruddy glow to their whiskered faces and hid the gaunt hunger traces that pinched their cheeks. From time to time they popped handfuls of black crickets into the boiling water, and, as soon as the insects stopped kicking, they scooped them out and devoured them.

That was the time when trappers and fur traders were tramping through this vast Western country of sagebrush-covered plains and towering snow-capped crags and peaks. When a man literally lived off the land and had to keep scratching to get both food and beaver pelts. It was a time of which Joe

2

Meek wrote: "I have held my hands in an ant hill until they were covered with ants, then greedily licked them off. I have taken the soles off my moccasins, crisped them in the fire, and eaten them. . . ."

Of course, the things of which Joe Meek tell are the extremes. It wasn't all like that even in the earliest days. There was wild game—elk, deer, mountain sheep, goats, buffalo. And there were Indians. It was from the Indians that the mountain men learned the eating customs of the country. They learned to take the marrow bones from a buffalo, crack them open, and melt down the rich yellowish fat into a form of butter. They learned to take a chunk of short ribs and roast it standing on end in front of a fire. They had sun-dried meat, too, pounded into fine pieces, mixed with tallow and mountain berries, which they called pemmican.

All this, and more, they learned from the Indians. But the main thing they learned was that they had to eat to live and a man couldn't be too particular. The closest they came to becoming gourmets was after they had made a big kill and there was plenty of meat for a feast. Then, no matter where they were—under the cool shadow of a great pine-forested mountain or in a protective coulee on the sun-baked plains—they stuffed themselves until they could eat no more. If they had salt to put on their meat they were in the lap of luxury. Epicureanism was out of place. A man who had hungrily licked up ants and crickets would feel silly tickling his throat with a peacock feather dipped in olive oil to make more room so he could feast again.

Thus the eating customs of the West were born and the struggle for existence in a rigorous life has kept them alive in lessening degree to this day. It's a common Western saying that bears no hint of approval for gourmets: "Some people live to eat, I eat to live."

The average Westerner in whom Epicureanism arouses a feeling of shame came by such morals honestly. The gold rushers began their toil when the first glance of the sun brought a rosy blush to the topmost mountain peaks, and they kept at it until it was too dark to see. They wrested their livelihood and their wealth, too, by dint of hard labor in the extreme. They could not afford to spend too much time over food. As Conrad Kohrs, who ran a butcher shop in the Alder Gulch diggings in Montana in 1863, the year the miners took complete control from the fur traders, wrote:

> Our work was considerably increased by our having to convert the entire beef into steak. The miners cooked their own victuals and because they wanted something that could be prepared quickly, there was little sale for boiling beef or other cheaper cuts. Steaks brought a good price and as all scraps, head, liver, etc. were worked up into sausage, there was no waste.

The cattlemen, like the miners, also had work to do. A cowboy who claimed he had to put in a twenty-six-hour shift, because he had to work all day, which was twenty-four hours, and two hours each night in addition, had no time to indulge in the glories of taste sensation. He had to "fill up and git." So you found canned milk and butter on the old time cow ranches from eastern Colorado to Oregon was a luxury. Here, too, meat, in the form of beef, was the standby, and ham and eggs, because of their rarity, were a treat.

Nevertheless, out of this welter caused by the struggle to change what was termed in the 1840s "The Great American Desert" into a place of habitation have come certain eating and drinking habits, molded by the past and colored by the present, that are distinctive to this vast, sprawling Western territory. They started with the necessities of the past and have been blended with the Old World customs of immigrants and the developments in older parts of the United States. And they have been restricted and shaped by the ever-present fact that there has been work to do and too much time can't be spent on food.

4

It's true that the miners and cattlemen who made their stake tried to settle down to a life of ease in which food and drink were accentuated. But they didn't know how. Neither do the Western chambers of commerce that deem a pie a success if it is the biggest ever baked, and that measure the success of their barbecues not by the taste of the food, but by the number of pounds and tons consumed and the number of persons served. Most of the restaurants in the cities don't know how, either. They are too busy striving to acquire what they have been told is éclat and developing a bastard French cookery. Yet, along the byways and in retreats away from the artificial limelight are the cookery and drinking customs of the people—a culture that like Topsy, just growed. It is here that the West may be seen as it is and it is this we will attempt to describe.

Miners' Concoctions

GO TO DENVER, COLORADO; BUTTE, MONTANA; BINGHAM, UTAH; KELLOGG, IDAHO; RENO, NEVADA; SACRAMENTO, CALIFORNIA. Go to Leadville, Tonopah, Cripple Creek. Go anywhere in the West where the heavy hand of the pick and shovel has molded living conditions and you will find similarity. You will find meat and potatoes—big, thick steaks, rare enough to weep—and you'll find your whiskey straight. Beer's all right to quench your thirst; but whiskey—ah, there's a lift, me bye. It cuts the dust from your throat and makes you feel like a man again.

Of course, it's not all that primitive now. Lots of the natives cut their whiskey and drink highballs called "whiskey and ditch." The ditch refers to the plain water that tumbles down the flumes from mountain drifts and is

5

measured in miner's inches. Lots more of them drink the fancy concoctions that outlanders have brought in, such as Cuba Libres (Coca-Cola and whiskey), Singapore Slings, and Zombies, where they shoot the works with everything. Some even drink Pink Ladies. Many have salads, greens, prepared breakfast foods, and other items termed "rabbit food." Actually, because of motion pictures, radios, newspapers, and magazines with their accompanying advertisements, any of the standardized foods found elsewhere can be found in the mining camps of the West. It's not that this food isn't to be had or even that it's spurned. It's just that the accent is on the lusty and vigorous.

The first thing a waitress hears when she goes on shift in the morning in a mining camp hash house is "a stack of hots." And that's the last thing her associates on the late shift hear at night. Once in a while a stinger, hog-head or tallow pot, working on a railroad hauling ore cars, varies it with a call for "a string of flats." But that's the exception. The usual is a stack. And what stacks!

A white-aproned male cook stands back of the counter and as fast as the waiter yells his order pours the white puddles of paste in perfect circles on the grid. Every move is practiced—just the proper tilt to the pitcher of rich batter, just the proper twist to get exactly the right amount on the stove. With practiced eye he watches the bubbling batter and, when the bubbles are just right, he flips over the disk to turn its golden-brown side upwards in smiling promise of the feed to come. Sausage, eggs, or ham is a favored complement. Savory, crisp hot cakes are served throughout the day and night. That is because the mines work three shifts a day and a miner may be having breakfast at anytime; also, hot cakes are frequently popular regardless of whether it is breakfast, dinner, or supper.

Many of these hash houses serve only dishes generally connected with breakfast; others are run in conjunction with bars and have a clientele composed almost entirely of men. Those who line their counters are a conglomerate assortment in nationality and dress. A miner fresh from the diggings with overalls and open-necked shirt might be perched alongside of a businessman in a dapper double-breasted suit with harmonizing tie and handkerchief. The mining camp hash house is a great leveler, a truly democratic institution.

Because the Irish came first with the construction of the railroads, their necks cooked red from laboring in the hot sun; because an Irish lad is a stout lad, full of adventure and the desire to get ahead, the mining camps of the West are full of them. They came singly, leaving relatives behind to keep them bound to the Ould Sod, but they brought their customs with them and their robust eating habits. They came to the Hot Water country of Nevada; they followed Marcus Daly to Butte, Montana; they filtered through Colorado, Idaho, Northern California—anywhere that labor was needed, where a man could get ahead. With them they brought their Cousin Jacks and Cousin Jennies from the mines of Cornwall. The Welsh came, too, with their experience in the collieries and the smelters of the Old Country. And the Scotch had similar ideas. Later when these people began "to get ahead," laborers were brought in from the Balkan countries—Montenegrins, Croatians, Serbs, Slovenes. The Irish maids gave way to the Swedes and Norwegians. Other nationalities came in. The West was the place to get ahead—and they all left their mark.

Because of the great number of single men, boarding houses sprang up in the Western camps and it was in these places, rather than swank hotels, that the solid, practical eating habits developed. These were places like the Big Ship, The Mad House, and the Mullin House, famed in old Butte, whose male clientele was predominantly miners. These were to be found in every camp from California to Canada.

Here the Irish miners enjoyed their stirabout, a sweet, semiliquid gruel made from oatmeal mush and thinned with milk. This was all right with the

7

Scotch, too, and the others came to like it in time. The Big Ship had a cop-per pot with a chute attached, and the bowls of stirabout were filled by pulling a lever. Each boarder ate two or three bowls at a sitting, which pleased the proprietor no end as it cut down on their appetites for more expensive hot cakes or ham and eggs. A special cook, however, was required as the miners were most particular about the flavor. Stirabout is still so pop-ular that many miners carry it in their lunch pails underground. Some mix it with tea or drinking water. Often a large pinch of salt is added to prevent heat cramps while working in hot stopes or drifts. The practice of salting their beer also springs from the necessity of making up the deficiency of salt, sweat out in the hot boxes of the mines.

Another favorite food of the mining region is the Cousin Jack pasty, introduced by the miners from Cornwall. This tasty meat pie of beef, pota-toes, onions, and rutabagas or turnips mixed together and encrusted in a wrapping of pie dough, baked to a golden brown, is called "a letter from 'ome." It is even sold from baskets by young boys, and on many an occasion when a miner tarries too long in one of the bars of Butte or elsewhere it is a welcome letter indeed.

Boxty is important among the Irish, Welsh, and Cornish miners because it is supposed to bring strength to the males and fecundity to the females. The first milk taken from a cow after calving—a thick clabber-like sub-stance—is strained and mixed with eggs and cornmeal or flour. It is then steamed into a savory pudding, which has the appearance and consistency of cottage cheese with a sweet-sour taste. With families who own their own cow, boxty is an annual treat.

Christmas Eve is marked by the appearance of potato cakes. These are not the potato cakes of other communities where they mix mashed pota-toes with pancake batter. These are heaps of steaming hot potatoes, mashed into a dry meal and mixed with flour until a heavy, unleavened dough

8

results. Caraway seeds are added and the dough is rolled into a great slab from which triangular cakes are cut with a thickness of four inches across the base. They are baked to a rich brown, and later, when they are served split open and covered with slabs of golden butter, the rich odor rivals the taste itself and makes each mouthful a precious parcel.

Less luscious are the oaten cakes of the Scotch, Nova Scotian, and Irish miners. These jaw breakers are made from oatmeal, milk, and water, pressed into a cake and baked to ironlike hardness over an open fire. Nevertheless, they are popular and have carried the miners through many a depression.

Other nationalities, likewise, have their special dishes. At Christmas and during the time of the Mesopust, a celebration that precedes Lent, povitica and slivovica are prepared for Croatian and Serbian tables. A sweet dough, rolled to a thin sheet, is used in preparing povitica. A filling comprised of crushed walnuts, butter, eggs, and honey is spread over the dough, which is then rolled and baked. The finished job appears like a jelly roll and is eaten with slivovica, a brandy made from prunes.

The Scandinavians have brought their lutefisk and smorgasbord; the Italians, their spaghetti and ravioli; the Mexicans, their frijoles and chile con carne—all have contributed something and all have been assimilated. Even at Reno, Nevada, famous for divorces and some good Italian cafes, this assimilation may be noted. At one ravioli dinner the menu was comprised of chicken fried to a golden brown in deep fat, Italian spaghetti and ravioli, shoestring potatoes, and sarma, a Slav dish made from pickled cabbage leaves wrapped around a filling of ground meat and rice.

Probably the greatest centers of assimilation are the homes and boarding houses in the mining camps. You can't run a boarding house only for Irish, Finns, or Italians. You have to take all comers even if you can't please everyone. So you do the best you can. Picture a huge room filled with long tables covered with white cloths and laid with heavy plates, cups, and saucers that can defy the most ardent or reckless of pearl divers. The doors are thrown open and in comes a motley crowd of men.

Some, dressed in business suits, are freshly shaved and barbered, ready for an evening's outing. Others come "just as they are"—a stubble of beard, hair quickly and carelessly combed, flannel shirts, overalls or old trousers. There's a merry round of greeting while white-uniformed girls bring heaping platters of steak, roast, stew, potatoes, corn, stewed tomatoes, or whatever may be on tap for the meal. These platters and dishes are placed at regularly spaced intervals in front of the men and conversation ceases. The men do their own "reaching" and talk is confined to "Pass the bread," "Let's have some butter," and "How about the cream."

As the steam-laden air seeps in from the kitchen and the substantial odor of roast beef rises to mingle with the more subtle smells of vegetables and sauces and the tantalizing whiff of apple pie to come, these men subconsciously take on a feeling of brotherhood. Bound by a common purpose, they do not feel the need to talk and their sense of well-being makes them spiritually expansive. It is the closest many of them will come again to family life.

Many of the homes are similar to the boarding houses, except that they are on a smaller scale. Large families are the rule, and with robust appetites they range themselves at the table with Father at the head and Mother at the foot, nearest the kitchen. Food is brought in on heaping dishes and big platters, and here, too, everyone does his own "reaching."

If Mother has become socially conscious, Father puts his shirt on over his long woolen underwear; if not, he eats in the comfort of his undershirt. The children come to the table in various stages of dress. One son might appear in overalls, just as he came off shift, merely having stopped to wash his face and hands. Another son, who happens to have a "heavy date," will be dressed in the latest. The older women, unless they are going out immediately after the meal, usually wear aprons or house dresses. Generally, there is a younger daughter, still quite pretty, who scorns such garb and keeps her dress on what she considers a higher plane.

Most important duty in the homes, boarding houses, and cafes of a mining camp is "putting up lunch buckets." Some restaurants advertise, "Lunch Buckets A Specialty." The putting up of lunch buckets is a personal matter. Not only the miner's individual tastes, but his nationality is taken into consideration, and the waitresses of such camps at Butte develop an uncanny ability to remember the preferences of each.

The miners congregate underground in groups for the meal hour, and usually find a cool, dry place in the fresher air of the sills of the level, away from the dust and gases of the stopes and raises where they work. Each miner finds himself a clean, dry "lagging," a three-inch plank about six feet long and sixteen inches wide. This is propped up and made into a reclining seat, which at the conclusion of the lunch is converted into a bed. There is a standard joke: "Did ye git yourself a good, soft laggin', bye?"

Most of the tall tales attributed to the miners have had their origin at these lunch hour gatherings. And as varied as the nationalities of the miners, who might be native Americans from all points of the country, Finns, Irish, Serbs, Cornish, Swedes and Norwegians, Welsh, Canadians, Scotch, Manxmen, Cletermores, Italians, Poles, Mexicans, and perhaps an odd Chilean miner, and a few Fardowns (Ulstermen), are the foods laid out in front of them.

Conventional ham sandwiches, cake, fruit, and apple pie might comprise the contents of the Americans' buckets, while his Irish workmate might face the same array with one exception. The son of Erin would wash his food down, not with coffee, but with strong black tea fortified with stirabout.

In the Cornish miner's bucket would be a generous-proportioned pasty, and a few slices of yellow saffron bread—or it might be saffron buns. Either one would be interspersed with myriad currants or raisins. Black tea with cream and sugar would fill the thermos flask.

The lunch pails from Italian or Austrian homes are sure to contain homemade red-and-white mottled salami sandwiches with their throat-burning seasonings, a button of garlic, and perhaps a whole Bermuda onion. Inevitably, there is Italian claret, or "Dago red." That is, if some other miner has not found his way to the wine before the lunch hour. Hunting for "Dago red" is a popular underground sport.

The meal of the Finns might contain strips of sharp-smelling dried fish, or dried, hard pieces of "jerky," a home-cured, smoky-tasting, leather-brown venison. A delicacy highly prized by the Finns is a sausage prepared by pounding the marrow from venison bones, which is then ground up with the jerked meat and stuffed into casings made from the intestines of the animal. The sausage is soft and looks like a dark liverwurst. Unlike salami, it is not spiced. This is a holiday food to the Finns and is often passed around to the other miners.

The Scotch, Welsh, and Canadians crunch their solid oaten cakes, and on occasion eat slices of haggis, a heavy, steamed meat pudding, cooked in the stomach of a sheep. In the mines, the greasy, brown slices with streaks of fat are eaten cold.

The Mexicans eat hot-tempered frijoles and tortillas. The Serbs have thick, greasy chunks of boiled brisket of beef of the cheapest quality, enormous half loaves of bread shaped like cigars, and garlic and onions in quantity.

It is undoubtedly through these lunch hours, and the interchange of food articles among the workers, that has made the larger mining camps some of the most cosmopolitan of cities in their food tastes. The average housewife may include any of a dozen foreign foods in her weekly menu.

When the shift is over it's a Sean (Shawn) O'Farrell to quench your thirst

and cut the dust from your throat. The Sean O'Farrell is really two drinks for the price of one—a full "shot glass" of one-hundred-proof whiskey, followed by a pint-sized scoop of beer. It is a tradition of the copper mines of Butte, Montana, and served, in saloons that cater to the miners' trade, for ten cents a shot.

Sean O'Farrells are not served any hour of the day or night, but are reserved for the hours when the miners are coming off shift. To purchase one for a dime, the buyer must have a lunch bucket on his arm to prove that he is a bona fide miner.

The Sean O', as it is often termed, is the miners' cure-all for the fatigue of the working day. One Sean O' is a refreshing tonic. Three make a new man of the miner and bring him to the same point as the New Englander on a visit to the South, who drank five mint juleps and then offered to lick "any damn Yankee in the house."

Imitations of the Sean O'Farrell have bobbed up in other industrial centers where they are heretically referred to as "boilermakers," but the double drink apparently had its origin in Butte in the nineties.

During Prohibition the countless speakeasies continued to serve Sean O's, but the price was twenty-five cents and moonshine whiskey and home brew were substituted.

With repeal, the saloons revived the ten-cent price. In the *Miners Voice*, an organ published by the Butte Miners Union, space is given to a blacklist of the names of bars that have abandoned the practice.

But this life in the large camps and cities isn't all there is to the mining regions of the West. In the sweltering desert country of Nevada, prospectors, called desert rats, plod along behind the traditional burro. Far up in the mountains of Colorado, Idaho, California, Montana, Utah, and Nevada their comrades may be met on tortuous trails, identified only by their pack and prospector's pick. Closer to civilization, where there are roads, may be seen

14

old trucks and jalopies with high wheels that can clear the many ruts and boulders. These, too, may contain prospectors and their outfits. Here are the lonely men who lead the way to hidden riches; the mining camps follow.

The prospector's grubstake is based on the necessity of light, nonperishable, substantial foods that can be carried with little difficulty. Flour, bacon, beans, sowbelly, baking powder, tea, sugar, salt, pepper, and dried fruits have made up the gold hunter's grubstake since the fifties and sixties. And over the span of three-quarters of a century, the only change has been in price.

In 1886, William Pascoe, one of Montana's oldest old-timers, had $54,000 in gold dust. He wanted to buy a sack of flour, which was unobtainable in Butte City. At Highland City, a booming mining camp twenty-six miles away, there were a few sacks that could be purchased for one hundred dollars each. Pascoe, when interviewed by a Butte *Evening News* reporter in 1910, said that a grubstake to tide him over the Christmas holidays of 1866 cost him one thousand dollars in gold dust for bacon, beans, dried fruit, and liquor. Pascoe did not state the amount of the liquor bill, but it can be surmised that it was at least half of the total. The miner of that date, as well as now, insisted that the moist and dry articles on the grub list should strike a fifty-fifty balance.

A story in point is of two later-day Highland City prospectors, who, running short of grub, drew straws to see which would journey the distance into Butte City to replenish their food box. One, with a hundred dollars in his pocket, set out and in a day or so was seen by his partner to be trudging back over the hill with a filled gunny sack over his shoulder. Weary, the shopper entered the cabin and dropped his purchases on the table, a twenty-five pound sack of flour and a case of quart bottles of whiskey.

His partner gazed over the purchases reflectively. He hefted the liquor and then hefted the flour.

"Geez, partner," he objected. "What're you goin' to do with all that flour?"

15

The almost unbelievable sum of one thousand dollars for a week's food is no longer required, as Pete LaGue, who has spent forty years wringing a living from the reluctant gravel of the Highlands, tells. In 1937, he spent $19.20 at a chain store for the following items: two hundred pounds of flour, three pounds of tea, five pounds of coffee, twenty-five pounds of sugar, twelve pounds of salt pork, one can of pepper, six cans of tomatoes, one bottle of anchovies, and one gallon of liquor store whiskey.

The prospector's diet has changed little in seventy-five years, but the chain store delivered the order to within a few miles of LaGue's cabin.

The old-time prospector obtained his vitamins through his sense of "feelin'." "I feel like I should have me a mess of berries," or "It's nearin' time to git me a mess of dand'line greens."

A frying pan and coffee pot were, and are, the chief cooking utensils. Bacon and sourdough were usually fried together in the same pan, although an occasional prospector might own a Dutch oven. Enough beans were boiled at one time to last a week and then were warmed over in the frying pan for each meal.

Western pioneers, like the present-day prospectors, sheepherders and backcountry ranchers, had to take conditions as they were. Usually this meant a shortage of such refinements as yeast and baking powder. As a result, salt-rising bread was popular.

Mrs. H. S. Neal, who with her sister and brother-in-law ran a stage coach station at Green Horn near Helena, Montana, in 1868, tells of the adaptation of this popular New England recipe to local conditions. The bread was made every day as the station was forced to feed the coach passengers immediately upon their arrival. Consequently, there was always the unpleasant odor of the bread about the kitchen. In summer it was placed out of doors to rise, but in winter it was of necessity confined to the kitchen. Nevertheless, some measure of comfort came from the saying, "the worse the smell the better the bread."

16

Sourdough, however, was much more common. The sourdough jar of the prospector was never allowed to become empty. And he still follows the age-old rule of the mountain cook: "Add as much as you take out." Many prospectors use the same jar of "starter" for years. It acts as the leavening for the sourdough flapjacks or occasional batch of bread.

The doughy consistency and faintly sour taste of these foods is aptly described by the name of the leavening, "sourdough."

Oddly enough, few prospectors depend on game for their supply of meat. Perhaps they have a prairie chicken or a sage hen, or a few trout now and then. The average prospector hasn't the facilities to keep game, and he is usually too occupied with his work to take time out for hunting. Bacon is the standby, and when the supply is exhausted, the only thing to do is to travel to town for more.

This then is the fare of the miner out in the hills. When he works in a town, all this is changed.

Weddings and wakes were always a diversion for the people of the West. Both are the occasion of a feast and lots of drinking. In the mining camps especially, wakes are important because Death is an ever-present, though unbidden, guest.

Mourners at the all-night wakes held in the homes of the Irish miners over the dead are fed an early-morning feast, prepared and brought in by neighbors. The only item of the funeral banquet prepared in the home of the deceased is strong coffee. A few hours after midnight, on each of the two, and sometimes three, nights of the wake, long board tables are set up on horses. Friends of the bereaved family bring in their choicest linen, china, and silver. If the deceased was at all popular, as many as fifty mourners may be seated at the tables.

There is no stinting at the feast. Every woman in the neighborhood vies with her neighbor to bring food that will be outstanding. Great pans of hot biscuits, fresh home-baked bread, pies, cakes, salads of a half-dozen varieties, huge roasts of pork, veal, and lamb, baked ham, and sometimes turkeys, ducks, and geese are provided for the guests. The serving, carving, table setting, and dish washing are attended to by neighborhood housewives and their daughters. Cigars and, sometimes, clay pipes are passed to the male mourners. Although great quantities of liquor are often drunk, the talk is subdued, and the general attitude one of respect.

Wakes are so popular with some people that they do not deem it necessary to have even a remote acquaintance with the dead. A story is told of Togo, an inveterate wake-goer and linotype mechanic who might have worked, and probably did, on any newspaper in the Rocky Mountain region. Togo had invited one of the reporters out for an evening's entertainment. When he had finished his shift, washed, and slicked his bartender's lick into place with careful manipulation of comb and brush, he proceeded to the front office to get his guest.

"Where we going?"

"To Merkla's wake. You ain't seen anything if you ain't seen a Serbian wake."

"But I don't even know the guy."

"That's nothing. Neither do I. But the dead guy ain't going to squeal so you got nothin' to worry about."

The wake was held in the huge hall of the Ancient Order of Hibernians, rented to the Serbian family for this occasion. The body had been placed on a small dais in the center of the floor and banked with flowers—huge wreaths, including the usual "Our Pal—R. I. P."

In a smaller room, off the main hall, long tables had been placed against the walls. On these were whole hams, roasted legs of golden-brown pork, whole cheeses, stacks of sliced bread, bowls of pickles, salads, and other food. Underneath were jugs of whiskey, red claret wine, popularly referred to as Dago red, and an amber grappa that looked like discolored water but carried a voltage as powerful as dynamite. Here a crowd of men had gathered, deserting the corpse, except for a long, mournful fellow whose saddened appearance seemed accentuated by boredom. In contrast to the deserted appearance of the hall was the spirit of conviviality in the small room. Men munched thick sandwiches and washed them down with glasses of the various beverages. In one corner a furious argument over atheism and the hereafter was underway. In another corner a group was laughing uproariously at "smoking car" jokes. The party lasted until dawn erased the gloom in the big hall and groups of women started to arrive preparatory for the funeral. With their arrival, the wake changed to a dignified, saddened affair.

When the prospector in the hills or the miner in the camp strikes it rich he wants to spend his money. He wants to make up for all the privation and hardships he has gone through in one hell-roaring binge. If he has taken on a woman as a partner he gets the benefit of expert advice. Women, even if they don't know what they are talking about, are a prolific fount of "swell ideas." But if he is a lone wolf, his range is limited. His gullet is his main source of pleasure, with his bed furnishing the only remaining variation. Even then the eternal female plays her part. But it is with his gullet that we are herewith concerned.

The story of the Last Chance Gulch miner who made his stake is a fine example of the lone wolf in action. He rode his pack horse up to the most deluxe restaurant in what is now the capital of Montana, and startled the tuxedoed waiters by demanding, "Bring me a hundred dollars worth of ham and eggs and a bale of hay for my horse."

Most of the mining magnates, however, who cut a wide swath through gold, silver, and copper camps of the West, rode tandem. This gave them a great advantage. Take Sandy Bowers of the Comstock country in Nevada, for instance. Sandy and his wife, the former Ellery Strong and later Eilley

19

Orrum of many fables, struck it rich. How rich they did not know. But they built a stone mansion a few miles south of Reno and made preparations to go to Europe to visit the Queen of England. They never got to see the Queen; she gave them the run around. But they ate their way through the best places of the East and abroad. And before they left Nevada they gave a party that was a rip-snorter. It was a catch-as-catch-can free-for-all at the gilded new International Hotel of Virginia City. It took place in the early 1860s, but they still talk about it in Nevada.

The party started its preparations weeks in advance. Sourdoughs from all over the Hot Water country laid out their best clothes. Some of them even trimmed their beards. Sandy started pack trains freighting across the Sierra from San Francisco, carrying the riches of champagnes, gifts, whiskies, seafood deluxe, and desserts. Every type of meat available, mostly beef and wild game, was prepared in various ways. The food, however, was incidental. As Sandy phrased it in his speech: "Thar's plenty of champagne, and money ain't no object."

That's the way it was throughout the West—from Virginia City, Nevada, to Central City, Colorado, to Butte, Montana—champagne was the symbol of riches and money was no object. Miners, who hadn't realized that their flannel shirts had a top button, struggled into boiled shirts and secretly fortified their courage with a few shots of red-eye. Then they sallied forth to guzzle champagne and eat oysters because that was the thing for a mining magnate to do.

Similar scenes were being enacted everywhere—men and women wanting the finer things of life and not quite knowing what the finer things were or how to get them. Up in Leadville, Colorado, H. A. W. Tabor built the Tabor Opera House in 1879 to match the Central City Opera House, opened the preceding year. It was another occasion for lavish parties featuring the symbolical oyster and free-flowing champagne. At the opening of the opera house, Tabor spotted the picture of William Shakespeare and asked who he was.

"Why, the greatest writer of plays who ever lived!"

"Well, what the hell has he ever done for Colorado!" roared Tabor. "Take it down and put my picture up there."

It mattered little that Tabor's appreciation of Epicureanism could be measured by his appreciation of literature—thar was plenty of champagne and money was no object.

In Anaconda, Montana, where Marcus Daly had built the world's largest copper smelter, he also erected the Montana Hotel. His attitude was exemplified in his remark as he stood across the street and viewed the three-story structure: "It looks like hell. Put on another story." So Anaconda, a town of three thousand in the 1880s, had one of the largest hotels west of the Mississippi.

Daly made the barroom an exact replica of the bar in the Hoffman House in New York City. The Anaconda Club was organized, Negro waiters were imported from Gotham, and banquets were featured with menus decorated by nationally famous artists. Thar was plenty of champagne and money was no object.

In the Silver Bow Club at Butte and in the Montana Club at Helena, similar events were taking place. The Silver Bow Club and the Montana Club were equally palatial. Excellent oil paintings and murals were on the walls of the dining room of men who a few years earlier had been content to smack their lips over burned sourdough soaked with bacon grease from the bottom of a blackened frying pan. The membership qualifications were somewhat flexible, but money, and stacks of it, was a prime requisite. A man's father might have been a horse thief, but if the son had accumulated his pile, he was accepted and no questions asked.

The cuisine and the bar were important. If money could buy it, the imported stewards, chefs, bartenders, and waiters would have it on hand.

Some of the diners were extravagant to the point of absurdity, with even the menus hand painted by noted artists. Here is a menu of a dinner eaten at the Montana Club by men, some of whom had to sign their names with an X.

Green Sea Turtle   Blue Points   Amontillado

Hors d'oeuvres

Small Patties aux Satpicon

Baked Pokpano a l'Italienne   Potatoes Duchess

Sauterne

Celery   Queen Olives

Timbales of Chicken with Truffles

Filets of Beef a la Printaniere   Pontet Canet

And so on through course after course until Bent's Water Crackers and Roquefort cheese were brought to the sated members.

Sometimes the members invited cronies of their prospecting days to be their guests at the club. The contrast between the members in full dress and the guests in working clothes went unnoticed. One Butte miner's wife remarked after her husband had spent an evening at the Silver Bow Club as a guest of a former pal: "Sure, the old man isn't feelin' well this mornin'. He was up at the Silver Bow Club half the night with the millionaires, fillin' his belly up with biled oysters and drinkin' champagne wine out of the painted ladies' slippers."

On one occasion at the Montana Club one of the members hired an old Chinese mining camp cook to prepare the food for a party he was giving.

Boiled beans, bacon, and sourdough biscuits were served to the guests who, in the past, were no strangers to this sort of fare.

The Montana Club and the Anaconda Club are still functioning, and in many instances the members are the sons, grandsons, and even great-grandsons of the founders. The Silver Bow Club has returned to the men who dig in the earth. The building, including banquet rooms, bar, painting, and ballrooms, was purchased by the Butte Miners Union, and in the club that once twinkled with the jewels of the millionaires' wives, the miners on Saturday evenings hold a jitney dance.

Even the mines themselves are used for dining rooms in Butte when special guests are to be entertained. One such affair took place on the 2,100-foot level of the West Steward Mine. The guests were the members of the Massachusetts Street Railway Association. The menu used names of ores, mines, and mining terms for the various foods. Such items as Shirt Bosses' Advice (roasts), Dynamite Sticks (asparagus), Parrot Lode (chicken), Chalcopyrite a la Little Mary (lamb), and Good Ore (cakes) were served.

The banquet passed off successfully, and if the appetite of any guest was spoiled by the thought of so many million tons of rock above his head, he kept the fact to himself.

Out of this furious search for a paradise with its attendant houris has come a more conservative type of festive gathering. Today, it's not so desperate, hectic, and, maybe, colorful as in the past, but it's more stable. The wealthy continue to ape those of the East and West coasts, whom they look up to—but they are doing a better job. Clubs such as the Montana or Anaconda clubs might well be one of many to be found scattered throughout the nation.

Businessmen's clubs, too, are more standardized, and when such organizations as the Rotary, Kiwanis, Lions, Exchange, and the like gather at the local hotel or restaurant to eat and sing their group songs, it might well be a gathering, with but a few minor variations, in Bangor, Maine, Sauk Center, Minnesota, or Oakland, California. But the ordinary gatherings of the people of the West are something different. These are usually held out-of-doors. Miners, especially, have a passion for the wide, open spaces. As a result, picnics are of foremost popularity.

Dining in Open Spaces

EVERYONE GIVES PICNICS—PRIVATE AND ORGANIZATIONAL. Before elections the Young Democrats, the old Democrats, the Young Republicans, the old Republicans, and various other organizations, all gather out-of-doors for speeches, handshaking, sandwiches, coffee, beer, and whiskey. Some vary it with barbecues; others, with fish fries. But the main thing is to get out-of-doors. Any excuse will do. A picnic attracts the people of the West like flies to a honey pot.

Traditional food for the ordinary picnics, or family gatherings, is fried chicken, potato salad with plenty of onions, bread and butter, fruit, coffee, or beer. With the new thermos jugs it is even possible to carry a completely cooked dinner of meat and vegetables and serve it hot. But the most fun of all is to bring the ingredients or take advantage of what is to be had in the surrounding country and cook the food yourself.

One of the favorite sports of young people during the fall months in the Philipsburg, Montana, mining country is to go on what they call "chickerees." A raid is made of a farmer's potato patch and chicken house. Then, a likely looking spot by a wooded stream is chosen and the picnic begins. The potatoes are washed clean and placed in cans filled with dry sand so that they are packed on all sides. The cans are then put in the open fire. The chickens

24

are cleaned and either placed on spits made from sharp pieces of sweet wood for broiling or are wrapped in wet pieces of newspaper or cloth and placed on the hot coals for roasting. The results are dry, mealy baked potatoes without the burnt, charred skin that makes plain roasted potatoes unpleasant and a golden-brown bird that is fit for a king. Salt and butter as well as coffee and cream are always carried along by the boys and girls who take part. The crisp mountain air and the piquant aroma of broiled chicken adds much to the affair, which started in a daring adventure accentuated by the darkness of night and the low whispering of the pines.

Not all of the young people's adventures are outside of the law. Most of them bring their food from home for the occasion—wieners or steak to be broiled on the end of a stick, marshmallows to be toasted, and beer or pop to wash it down. A favorite trick is to take chunks of beef and pork and alternate them on a sharpened stick. The whole is toasted over the fire and eaten with onions.

University of Nevada students are especially eager for their "beer picnics." These follow the general rule of food and drink. After satisfying their hunger they sit around the fire singing songs and drinking beer. An equal number of boys and girls attend, dressed in all types of slacks, corduroy pants, and sweatshirts. Many a romance has blossomed under the romantic spell of the pines enhanced by the tantalizing odor of sweet-burning wood mingled with that of broiling steaks or hot dogs.

Fish fries and barbecues are popular in the mountain country. The barbecues are different from those of the plains, with their cattlemen's tradition and flavor of Texas and the Southwest. The background of the mountain barbecue comes farther. It comes from the Old Country, in Yugoslavia or Serbia, where fiercely mustached peasants broiled whole sheep carcasses over the open fire, washed the thick sandwiches down with wine red as the grapes of their native land, and topped it off with grappa, amber and

25

fiery as the burning sun.

Among the cattlemen, it's beef. But mutton is a favorite in the mountains. There are no women here; this is a man's party. It starts early in the morning when several of the young men go to a selected spot beside a stream of cold, sparkling water. Although usually led by a Croatian or youth of Slavic descent, today in the Rocky Mountains all nationalities participate. No pit is dug, but a huge fire is made and kept burning until the wood is reduced to coals. A whole sheep is then lashed to a long pole, which is placed on tripods at each end so that it can be turned continuously. The master of the barbecue is an autocrat of assured position. Take Whitey for instance.

Whitey was young, but he knew his stuff. He had learned it from his father, who had come to Wallace, Idaho, from some mountain village in Yugoslavia. Whitey had been born in Wallace and was American to the core. He had picked up all the Americanisms of one eager to definitely prove that he belongs. As a result, his methods of preparing the barbecue were a mixture of the Old Country and the new.

The sauce that he prepared was definitely Old Country. There was a faint touch of garlic and a mixture of spices and herbs that were a mysterious secret as far as the others were concerned. But Whitey's methods were Western, picked up from *Western Story* magazines, books, and conversation with cowboys who had drifted into the mining city from time to time from the outlying cow country. He was gruff and dictatorial, but he was capable of turning a sheep into a golden-brown, aromatic offering to the great god Hunger. He was in supreme command because of his knowledge of the composition of the mysterious sauce, and he knew it.

"Turn it over slowly. Do you think you are at a race? That's too slow, do you want to burn it?"

Thus he stormed and fired orders, while the faces of his helpers red-

26

dened and little trickles of sweat ran down their cheeks to collect and drip from their noses and chins. From time to time he took a stick, one end of which had been wrapped with a cloth, and dipped it in the sauce, which he carefully daubed over the sheep. As the mutton roasted a tantalizing odor pervaded the pine-wooded grove.

Whitey's helpers spelled each other off from time to time to keep the sheep steadily rotating. Occasionally, when Whitey left the scene, one of them would slip out a knife and, at risk of burned fingers, would rip off one of the almost done edges of meat and hastily cram it in his mouth. Whitey didn't approve of this; he wanted everything just so. When the others would arrive he didn't want to greet them with a gouged and hacked-up hunk of meat; he wanted a golden masterpiece, unmarred and awaiting the knife with virginal completeness.

After several hours the coals of the fire began to turn to heaps of gray ashes. These, however, remained hot enough to continue the cooking process at a slower rate, even though the cottonwood grove was perceptively cooling. It was then that another carload of youths drove up. They piled out with hungry shouts and cheers for Whitey, unloading loaves of bread, cases of beer, and jugs of wine and grappa. All except the bread was placed in the creek to keep cool. Then the gang gathered around the fire watching the sheep turning on its improvised spit.

"How long is it going to take? Is it done yet Whitey? We're all hungry as hell."

Whitey moved with tantalizing slowness, giving them no satisfaction. The odor of roasting mutton enhanced by the faint smell of garlic and spices aggravated their eagerness. Soon a couple of them, unable to wait longer, began handing out slices of bread. Whitey remained unhurried, drawing the last full measure of enjoyment from his tantalizing slowness. At last he ordered the tripods moved back and with a sharp butcher knife began

27

cutting off slices of meat. He had a plate nearby, but he never got to use it.

"Just slap it on this piece of bread, Whitey."

Eager hands thrust toward him formed sandwiches as fast as Whitey could serve. A few ravenous gulps and they were back for more. It seemed like the parade would never end, but Whitey glowed and expanded under the pressure. He seemed almost sad when he got ahead of the gang and was able to take a heaping plate of meat with several loaves of bread and join them on the bank of the creek where they had already uncorked bottles of wine, grappa, and beer.

From then on it was a hilarious party—Croatians, Serbs, Irish, Scandinavians—eating, drinking, and wisecracking in the American manner; segments of this culture, portions of that, all put together in a new and original way.

The fish fries vary from small affairs where two or more men on fishing parties fry their catch over an open fire to huge gatherings sponsored by sportsmen's associations. These huge gatherings in the sparsely settled sections of the West enable old friends to renew acquaintances and politicians to meet their constituents personally. "Talking shop," reminiscing, and talking politics are the order of the day.

No formal invitations are issued to these affairs; everyone knows he is welcome and everyone takes the attitude that it is his party. They start arriving early in the morning—by automobile, horse and buggy, wagons, horseback, or on foot. The sportsmen's committee is already at hand and at work.

White-aproned men stand back of serving tables erected by laying planks over sawhorses. These tables are loaded with great pots of potato salad dappled with pieces of onions and savory with seasoning and mayonnaise. Long platters, bright with freshly sliced white bread; plates of pickles and sliced onions; jars of mustard; bowls of butter; cans of condensed milk; and salt and pepper shakers are scattered here and there.

Farther back of the tables other white-aproned men are busy at a large fire over which sections of steel rails had been placed to form a grill. Here the trout is being fried. Boned sections, rolled in flour are dipped into smoking skillets of bacon grease, later to be lifted out, richly browned and crisped. Smaller fish are fried just as they are after they have been cleaned, but with the heads still attached. Many claim that this sized fish carries the sweetest meat. At smaller gatherings the fish are fried with strips of bacon placed either inside or attached to the outside with toothpicks, but at the larger fries, bacon grease suffices.

Nearby are smaller fires on which huge pots of water are being brought to a boil, ready for the making of coffee. Freezers, full of ice cream, generally stand in a shaded spot.

When enough fish has been fried so that the cooks are certain of keeping ahead of the hungry mob, the cry, "Come and get it," peals forth, accompanied by the pounding of steel against steel, and everyone rushes to fall in line. The clear mountain air already has whetted their appetites, and as they file past the tables the tantalizing smells of bacon and frying fish boost them to greater heights. The smoke from sweet-wood fires mingling with the perfume of wildflowers and pine trees catches up the food odor, diluting and blending it into something that can only be captured out-of-doors.

As soon as the people are served they pick shaded, grassy spots and continue their visiting over the plates of food. There's something about crisp-fried trout, glistening and golden in the sunlight and flanked with creamy heaps of green-speckled potato salad that lifts such a meal from the prosaic to the sublime when it is cooked and eaten out-of-doors. Probably, it's the outdoor smell that does it; but it is something to be remembered, and a Westerner will travel miles to a fish fry.

Along the West Coast and near the Columbia River the fish fry takes on

more pretentious proportions—as far as menu is concerned—and becomes a beach party or shore dinner. Here, too, however, the picnic idea or outdoor gathering holds its supremacy.

Along the Columbia River in Washington and Oregon the salmon reigns supreme. He has been king since the days when the Chinook Indians ceremoniously carved and cooked the first catch of the season, making certain that they feasted before sunset and that the heart was never thrown back into the river, eaten by dogs, or mutilated.

Anywhere in Oregon or Washington, in the vicinity of the Columbia, a salmon barbecue might take place. It may be at Yachats or on the San Juan

Islands, but wherever it is, it is always an affair of major importance.

In Yachats, a local character known as Dunk, a shortening of the name Dunkhorst, brought a touch of old Germany to the barbecue. Dunk dissolved brown sugar in a big tub of water and soaked the salmon in the solution. When the fish were barbecued they "had something," and ever since the housewives of Yachats have been washing their salmon in water sweetened with brown sugar.

Barbecued salmon are usually placed in a barbecue pit and covered with ferns or grass. In addition to barbecuing, salmon is cooked by frying as steaks, baking, creaming, or used in salads. It is frequently jerked or smoked and served with beer.

Oregon, and especially Portland, where The Quelle Restaurant in earlier days made a feature of the dish, is famous for its crawfish dinners. In Portland they still tell how William Howard Taft ordered several dozen sent to his hotel suite and how Kolb and Dill, the comedians, gave crawfish parties at The Quelle every night.

Crawfish are served with pickles, cheese and crackers, and mugs of beer that are filled and refilled time and again. The procedure of eating is somewhat of a rite and described as follows:

> First you twist the finials from the end of the tail, and elevating the crawfish and throwing back your head, you quickly suck the soup from the end of the tail, which acts as a straw. Next you lift the large shell off the body and scrape out with a knife (the only implement used) a gooey-looking substance which you spread on a cracker— caviar never tasted like this! If it is the season for eggs you are doubly lucky. Your neighbor who doesn't find any eggs drools with envy.
>
> Finally you twist off the large claws and crack them with your hands or your teeth and eat the delicious white meat. Large checked dish

31

towels are used for napkins and since manners are neither possible nor desirable, you make as much noise and eat as fast as possible.

The story goes that the recipe for cooking crawfish originated in Portland one day in the nineties when Herr Kummli, chef of the Portland Hotel, and Max Schmidt, owner of the Vienna Café, were having tea, or possibly schnapps, with Fred and Louis Sechtem, owners of The Quelle, and a fisherman brought in a sack of crawfish for sale.

Schmidt recalled that in Germany they were cooked in salt water flavored with caraway seed. They tried this method but the crawfish were flavorless. The other cooks suggested adding various ingredients, onions, bay leaf, and allspice, but the crowning touch came when Father Sommer of the German Catholic Church dropped in and suggested putting white wine in the mixture.

For real outdoor sport, however, there's nothing like a geoduck (gweduc) hunt. This large clam, which averages from one-and-a-half to two-and-a-half pounds in weight, was placed under the protection of the Washington Fish and Game Law in 1931. A limit of three geoducks per person per day was set and a restriction of no tools other than "fork, pick or shovel, operated by hand by one person for personal use" was set. Furthermore, it was decreed that no person should "at any time, maim or injure any Geoduck or thrust any stick or other instrument through the neck or body of such geoduck before digging." Thus the geoduck hunt entered the realm of genuine sport.

The first thing to do is to select a good shady beach when the tide has gone out. With sharp eyes you might spot one of the clams spouting water and sand. There's where the shovel comes in and you'd better come in with it fast—very fast; because no matter how fast you are, the geoduck is likely to be that much faster. He can dig like a small-town gossip on the scent of a secret marriage. And, unless you have marked well the spot where he was seen, you're likely to miss him.

Some of the old-timers in the Puget Sound district mark the spot by pushing a section of stovepipe down over the clam's neck and digging around it. But even that is tough because the geoduck is very sensitive to footsteps and goes for cover at the least provocation. The Puget Sound Indians used a fish hook on a pole to snag the geoduck's neck and hold him while they dug. But, since the legislative action of 1931, that's out, and you have to give the geoduck an even break.

When enough of the clams are accumulated for a feast you can either go indoors or start the party right there on the beach. The beach is preferable if you have any shred of romance—and most Westerners, hard-boiled though they may seem, are romanticists at heart. There on the beach where the wind is washed by the sea and the singing waves furnish luncheon hour music, a fire is built from dried driftwood. Water is brought to a boil and the clams are plunged in for a scalding.

After this scalding is completed the soft shell is cut away, the geoduck is cleaned, and a thin layer of skin that encrusts the clam is scraped off. The meat is then cut into thin slices, rolled in egg-and-breadcrumb batter and fried in deep fat. With potato chips, olives, pickles, a tart relish, crackers, and beer—there's a feast. With the salt-sea air seasoning the aroma from the frying clams, that greatest sauce of all—hunger—is stimulated to an almost unbearable degree. Then, when the clams are served with their salty complement of potato chips, a thirst is induced that makes the frothy beer taste like something very special, indeed. With a meal like this amid the approving laughter of the waves, it's no wonder that the entire party stretch out in scanty bathing suits on the warm beach to bask in the sun, confident that "God's in his Heaven and all's right with the world."

And that isn't all that's to be had in this Pacific coastal country. There's the Olympia oyster, the delightful taste of which saved the Washington state capital for the town of Olympia when its citizens sent a special train to serve these oysters without charge to the state's voting population.

These oysters are popular throughout the Western country. Go into any bar in the Rocky Mountain region and you will find small bottles of prepared Olympia oyster cocktails nestled seductively in a bed of chipped ice. If you've had a hard night and need a lifter-upper without running the danger that it might turn into a layer-downer, order one. The biting Worcestershire and Tabasco sauce, blended into the thick tomato puree, will tone up your stomach and the oyster, itself, will give strength to your cause. You can go to see your Aunt Harriet or drop into the boss's private office and look either one in the eye. Or, if you've reached that sated condition where you're ripe for a hemlock potion, try an Olympia oyster pepper-pan roast. There's no room for hemlock in this highly seasoned dish that tickles the nostrils and sends the hot blood coursing through the body. There's more spiritual uplift in this dish than in all the sweatered females in Hollywood.

Yes, there's crab, cod, halibut, tuna, sturgeon, and myriad others. And there's clambakes, fish fries, and oyster roasts. All this, and salmon, too. Maybe it's the economic status of salmon, as some claim, that places it in its pre-eminent position. But, be that as it may, the crown-touch of the Oregon State Pioneers' annual dinner is the parade of the salmon. One pioneer describes it as follows:

By salmon I don't mean just any old salmon. I mean our Columbia River salmon, nice an' firm an' red-meated. There ain't any better fish anywhere—maybe I'd better say there ain't as good fish anywhere—as our Columbia River Chinook. Whenever us Oregonians want to do something specially nice for anybody, like the

34

President of the United States, or some other bigwig, we give him one of them grand fish. Of course we will have some ham an' chicken, but, as I was sayin', the salmon's the big thing—bigger 'n more ways than one. Baked whole, with nice strips of bacon laid across it so it won't stick to the roastin' pan—'course I mean after it's cleaned and the scales scraped good with a sharp knife—them baked salmon sure is a pretty sight. The waiters—sons and daughters, mind you—carry them in a procession 'round the tables for everybody to see. Used to be there was a long procession of 'em, all of 'em with a salmon maybe three feet long, crisp and shinin' an' decorated with parsley. Then, after everybody had a look, they'd take the salmon to one of the booths, where it was dished out in portions, with the best hot cream-and-egg sauce you ever tasted.

In the state of Washington the salmon is looked upon with such veneration that Chief William Shelton's annual salmon feast at Tulalip is attended by the most distinguished men of the state. An invitation to the chief's dinner, which is prepared by the Indian women of the reservation and served in the Indian manner, is the equivalent of the accolade with Excalibur in the hand of King Arthur, himself.

The little cousin of the salmon—the smelt—comes in for its share of adoration. When the run is on in the early spring in the Columbia and its tributaries, millions of the silvery little fellows are trapped. A quick lip lengthwise with a sharp knife removes the viscera and the backbone. The fish is then rolled in cracker meal and popped into a pan of smoking grease—and there's a real dish. Thousands gather on the Cowlitz River to feast on fried smelt served by the most beautiful girls of the town of Longview in honor of the annual run.

Community Gatherings

BECAUSE OF THE SMALL SIZE OF MOST WESTERN COMMUNITIES, AND BECAUSE THE FOUNDING OF THESE COMMUNITIES IS SO RECENT THAT MANY OF THE ORIGINAL SETTLERS ARE STILL LIVING, COMMUNITY GATHERINGS TO FEAST AND FROLIC HAVE BECOME A SOLIDLY ROOTED CUSTOM. This custom has its origin in pioneer times when trappers from an area larger than a dozen or more Eastern states combined would gather at the fur traders' rendezvous on Green River in Wyoming for orgies of eating and drinking so wild and robust that the Roman God Bacchus would have hesitated to attend. The orgies disappeared with Uncle Dick Wooten and his Taos Lightning, a particularly potent drink from the New Mexico settlement. Today, the basic reason for these gatherings—the gregariousness of human nature and especially of the Westerner to whom crowds are a novelty to be enjoyed for their sake alone—survives and continues to make the community gathering important.

Up at the Plymouth community, three miles west of Corvallis, Oregon, the farmers get together several times each year for a "home-talent" program of recitations, songs, skits, and dancing. Six-year-old Jenny rumples the hem of her stiffly starched white dress while she tells the audience that she is "a little daffodil, peeping forth so bright." And her proud mother squirms with bubbling pride at her success and writhes in abject misery at her failure. But however it is viewed from the outside, it is important. It is an exchange and a communion.

So, too, is the dancing that follows. The rhythm of the fiddle, wailing out "Michigan Girl" and "Skip-to-My-Lou", is important as well. It is the rising crescendo. But the crowning point of all is the luncheon that follows. It

36

is the peak that tops off all sensual pleasures. Here are the large bowls of potato salad, the rich brown bean loaf; the darker, but more spicy, meat loaf; the Jell-O puddings and cookies; pickled beets; sweet, sour and dill pickles; jams and jellies; and the variety of cake.

Apple-cheeked women in gingham dresses bustle around, their ample breasts exuding maternal hospitality. Excited children and more placid men in freshly washed denim eye the tables with restrained eagerness. The mingled odors of hot food whip up their appetites. But amenities are short—they are there to eat.

"That's mighty fine meat loaf, Mrs. Roland. Hey, Jim, have you tried that potato salad in the big, blue bowl? Don't miss it."

Mrs. Roland and the maker of the salad in the big, blue bowl beam their pleasure. There's a competition at these affairs that is subtler than that of satisfying the appetite for food. These rural housewives work their hardest to achieve that something that lifts their offering from the commonplace. Success is food for the soul.

And so it is throughout the rural West—in country schoolhouses, church basements, lodge halls—the picture is the same. Sometimes it varies from a plain country dance to possibly the presentation of an amateur drama, but basically it is the same, just as it was basically the same at the trappers' and fur traders' rendezvous at Taos, New Mexico, and at Green River, Wyoming. It was and is the feast that counts.

Here, in these community gatherings, as in the boarding houses and homes of the smelter and mining camps, the blending of America's eating customs takes place. In Spokane, Washington, members of the Greek Orthodox Church entertain three thousand at a dinner, which is served on each of three succeeding nights. In Cheyenne, Wyoming, the Norwegians celebrate May 17, Independence Day, with a feast that includes lutefisk, pastejar, goat cheese, and sugar-sprinkled kafflebrod. In Frenchtown,

Montana, St. John the Baptist is honored with a celebration on June 24.

These celebrations are no longer foreign affairs, even though the national customs of the group in charge predominate. They have been too closely blended into America. Take the celebration at Frenchtown. Once, a person had to speak French to be able to enjoy it. Today, that is all changed; the conversation is bilingual.

The St. John's Day celebrations started in Frenchtown more than a half century ago. They are held on the Saturday closest to June 24. The day opens with the entire community attending mass in the morning. Then lunch is served—and what a lunch.

The main dish is roast chicken or turkey with dressing; not ordinary dressing, but dressing made in the French tradition brought to Montana from Canada. Instead of bread, potatoes are boiled and mashed. Ground pork is kneaded into this mealy mass and onion, salt, pepper, and sage— plenty of sage—is added along with the minced giblets. The dressing, much darker than bread dressing, flavors the fowl and adds pungency to the aroma, like the odor that arises from the sagebrush-covered Western plains on a hot August day.

Fluffy white mashed potatoes, golden sweet potatoes, roasted in their jackets, and rich, brown gravy bolster the slices of chicken or turkey on the diner's plate. A salad of orange carrots mixed with green beans and molded into a yellow gelatin adds a splash of color that is supplemented by dishes of radishes, pickles, and celery. Ice cream and cake usually furnish the dessert, as pie is seldom served on St. John's Day. Sometimes a carrot pudding, made of ground carrots, potatoes, and raisins, steamed like the traditional plum pudding of the New Englanders and served with a hard brandy sauce, brings the meal to an end.

Outdoor sports add a round of gaiety to the afternoon program. Fat men and women quiver and shake as they force their blubbery bodies over a race course, much to the amusement of the spectators. There are potato, egg, cigarette, and sack races that combine skill with amusement because of the handicaps they impose on the participants. Horse races give many a thrill, and there's always the baseball game.

In the evening, a dinner, similar to the noon dinner except that it lasts longer, is served. Then comes the dancing. The Irish Washerwoman, polkas, and square dances turn the hall into a mad whirl of dervishes. "Ladies to the right; gents to the left." Dark eyes sparkling beneath long, black eyelashes. White flashes of teeth framed in red by beckoning lips. And in the kitchen, older women, patiently resigned, and young girls, hopefully waiting, wash and wipe huge stacks of dishes to make ready for the midnight lunch. They call it lunch, but it, too, is the equal of the noon and evening dinners.

Hours later, the wailing of the fiddles is strangled by the gray fingers of dawn and the celebrants return home, tired but happy. It's a robust celebration by a robust people, grown strong through wresting their livelihood by sheer force from an unwilling soil. But it's typical of the rural West, which works hard, plays hard, and eats heartily.

The St. John's Day celebration is an example of a major event, but throughout the year, and especially in the winter, are the country dances. These are just as robust, albeit on a smaller scale.

In the kitchen—and there is usually a kitchen where an oil stove is a fixture—is an array of food—sandwiches of all kinds, meat, cheese, egg, and peanut butter; cakes of many shapes and colors (the ones who prepare the lunch eye the cakes, and it is a compliment to the cook whose cake is reserved to the last); pickles, of course—sweet, sour, and dill—something easily parceled out—not relishes; salads with their unknown ingredients; and last, but not least, the coffee, which has already been measured out and tied in bags and is starting to heat in the big kettles provided for the purpose.

The music starts and the dance is on. Couple after couple joins the circling crowd, and spirits wax exuberant. When the number is finished the men congregate, discussing crops, livestock, and maybe the latest scandal; the women seek the benches or gather in groups, exchanging banter and witticisms along with commonplace items. The music starts again and they are whirled away by different partners. Those remaining on the benches or in the hallways study the scene before them, missing very little.

At twelve o'clock all line up, either sitting or standing. The paper plates and napkins are passed; the tin cups, forks, and spoons follow. The first sandwiches appear. Then the salads, pickles, and cake. A man comes along carrying the heavy pot of coffee and pours it, steaming, into the cups so carefully held out. Someone follows with cream and sugar. Merrily the people talk, laugh, and eat. Second helpings are generously offered until everyone is more than satisfied.

More groups gather and visiting is renewed. The floor, by this time, is not so smooth and shiny. Someone may start across it with a brush, clearing away the litter, and new wax may be scattered. This is usually the signal for the orchestra to start again, and several hours of dancing follow. "Home Sweet Home" is played, sleepy children rounded up, wraps collected, cars started up, and farewells shouted; and the hall is left in all its disarray, to be cleaned up next day in readiness for another dance in the not-so-faraway future.

This is a scene that might take place in the redwood clearings of northern California, dry-land farms or rich, irrigated agricultural areas of Nevada, Utah, Colorado, Wyoming, Idaho, Montana, Washington, Oregon—in wheat country, on the cattle and sheep range, any place in the West. Here, the meal

40

is of prime importance, but the food is not. These people do not need imported caviar or lobster a la Newburg to regale jaded appetites. They have had to live off the land where ingenuity and creative ability that sometimes has approached the peak of brilliance has kept them from sinking under the banalities of mediocre cookery.

Creative Cooking

WHEN WE THINK OF PIONEERS WE THINK OF HOMERIC FIGURES IN A HAZY, DISTANT AGE. But throughout the West are country school teachers instructing classes of three, four, and five pupils; homesteaders and small ranchers, whose nearest neighbor may be five miles away; small miners; stump farmers; prospectors; and other lonely figures. These people are living a pioneer existence today, lifting their lives from the prosaic by their creative ability in molding the materials they have on hand.

Consequently, in the West you may, at the right season of the years be served with a luscious elderberry pie, its crust browned and flaky from a shortening of bear grease and the deep blue berries oozing a thick juice with a tartish-sweet flavor all their own. Or you might sit down to a broiled venison or elk steak and be offered "ketchup" made from buffalo berries picked right after a frost when they are a bright red and full flavored. These berries are boiled and the juice is blended with salt, pepper, mustard, vinegar, garlic, and spices to form a delicious and zestful sauce. Chokecherry syrup gives a decided lift to sourdough hot cakes or biscuits. Or the berries may be made into jellies and jams along with other berries such as gooseberry, wild currant, and many others. And, then, there's wine. Any of these

41

berries, and even the lowly dandelion, may be made into a beverage sure to add a merry lilt to a festive gathering.

Jam and jelly making is important to the people of the West. Housewives throughout this area "put up" fruits and berries as they come on the market from the fruit-growing sections of the Pacific Coast and lower altitudes of the mountain country. These are supplemented by native fruits such as the thorn apple, wild plum, strawberry, raspberry, serviceberry, and many others. Wild game and vegetables also are canned in season.

The life of these people is not entirely one monotonous round of fried beans, baked beans, boiled beans, and just beans, varied only by an occasional jack rabbit or two. Not as long as the creative ability of these Western people holds forth. The bean is often glorified into a bean loaf, brown and piquant with spices, garlic, or onion. Sometimes, when mashed, it might even be turned into a sweet called bean fudge. And until you have tasted jack rabbit mincemeat pie you have never appreciated true brilliance of creative ability. Here's the story of a young wife who had joined a Western homesteader in battling the soil:

One moonlight night we started from the house. We hadn't left the farm buildings far behind when a jack rabbit dashed by only to stop and sit up and gaze curiously at the light of my lantern. I circled cautiously until I was in line for a good shot. Rabbit after rabbit was killed until I realized to continue would be criminal.

The next day I decided to make mincemeat in the way my neighbors had explained. I cooked several of the rabbits until I was certain I had four pounds of rabbit meat. Then I chopped some citron fine, took some raisins, apples, spices, and a quart of hard cider, and made mincemeat. That afternoon I made pie. With my tongue in my cheek, I added a small extra glass of the cider to each pie. The cider had plenty of oomph, and so did the mincemeat. The pies came out of the oven, and they were the best I ever made.

In such manner are eating habits formed in the West—through trial and error and the complete cooperation of neighbor with neighbor in this sparsely settled country. And even with the lack of easily accessible food materials, the parties continue. Take this story of a young woman who invented what she called "Depression Cake" to take to a community Fourth of July picnic, rodeo, and general get-together:

Eggs! She had none. The few hens she possessed were either burdened with the responsibility of baby chicks, or setting on eggs, dispositions ruined and cross-eyed with chagrin over confinement and the hot weather.

Butter and milk! Ye Gods! Old Stubby had taken a leave of absence and followed a herd of whitefaces that were grazing over the West Fork, having observed a fine gentleman among them who appealed to her fickle heart. Ethel must remember to have Nick go after her right after the Fourth.

Ethel looked at the pan of raisins stewing on the stove. An idea entered her mind; it was worth trying, and she could experiment on her husband and brother. Necessity was the mother of invention.

When the raisins had partially cooled, she carefully measured a cup of the fruit and a cup of the juice and poured them into a mixing bowl, adding a teaspoonful of soda, half a teaspoonful of cinnamon and nutmeg, a pinch of cloves, ginger, and allspice. A heaping tablespoon of bacon drippings went in next, and she watched the mixture bubble and froth, wondering if the stuff would explode. She sifted one and three-fourths cups of common flour and a cup of

43

sugar, a pinch of salt, and a teaspoonful of baking powder, added them to the volcanic mass in her mixing bowl. After a moment of hesitation, she put in a teaspoonful of flavoring. What was it? A cake or pudding? She did not know.

After greasing and flouring a loaf-cake tin, she spread the batter in the pan, and, closing her eyes, prayed fervently as she closed the oven door on the mystery.

Forty minutes later Ethel opened the oven door, her eyes wide with wonder. Spices—no odor from the Old World ever smelled more delicious. The cake—for by all the Gods it was a cake—had risen, round, light, brown, shrinking away from the pan, proclaiming to the world that it was sufficiently baked.

No modern chef ever carried a brainchild more carefully or proudly than Ethel when she placed the cake to cool. Her creation appeared beautiful, but how would it taste?

When the men came in weary and hungry from work, they were greeted at the door with the odor of that cake, which held the place of honor in the center of the table.

"How?" asked the man of the house, well aware of the lack of provisions.

"Eat it first," answered Ethel. "I'm afraid to talk."

After the cake had been eaten to the last crumb, the brother inquired cautiously, "Gosh, Ethel, do you reckon you can do it again?"

Ethel nodded assent. The Fourth of July celebration was a success, and that's how "Depression Cake" came into being.

It is only natural, then, that these Western communities celebrate their success in conquering the soil with a festive gathering in honor of that for which the community is most famed.

44

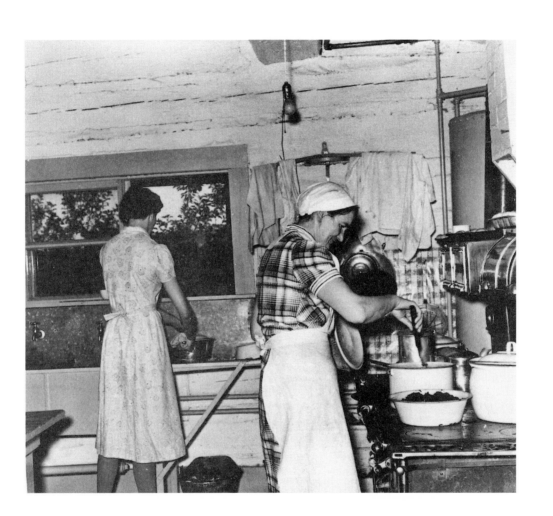

Specialty Festivals

IN WENATCHEE, WASHINGTON, IT'S THE APPLE BLOSSOM FESTIVAL, FEATURED BY AN ELABORATE ENTERTAINMENT OF PAGEANTRY AND PARADES, PLUS A GENERAL PICNIC IN THE PARK AND THE "LARGEST" APPLE PIE IN THE WORLD. At Long Beach they cook up the "largest" clam fritter in the world, using a truckload of clams. At the Marysville Strawberry Festival and at Bellevue the town's prettiest girls serve strawberry shortcake to all comers amid a program of general sports and dancing. Burlington in Skagit County, Washington, goes to the extent of building a specially constructed dish, eight feet long, four feet high and four feet wide, which is placed in the center of town to hold the "largest" ice cream sundae in the world, from which hundreds of people are served.

At Buckley, Washington, it's "Peach-a-Reno" Day with peach shortcake served to thousands. At Anacortes, Washington, the annual Mariner's Pageant features the barbecuing of King Salmon.

The same is true in Colorado as in Washington. Carbondale celebrates Potato Day with an exhibition of agricultural products grown in the Carbondale district. Rifle, Colorado, has its Apple Pie Day, and Pickle Day is important at Platteville. At Glenwood Springs there is an annual strawberry festival with free strawberries, cake, and ice cream. Rocky Ford celebrates its Melon Day when more than ten thousand watermelons and several thousand cantaloupes are distributed.

In Greeley, Colorado, there is the Spud Rodeo on the Fourth of July, and Greeley residents take great pride in their potatoes, which they term "the finest in the world." Then they explain why newcomers to the state have trouble cooking the tuber:

It is not the potatoes that misbehave, but it is the altitude behaving quite normally. And the situation is true of not only potatoes, but of cakes, and beans and beets and turnips—in fact, of any food requiring heat. Water boils at 212 degrees at sea level. In Colorado, and the other Rocky Mountain states where the air is much lighter, water boils at 202 degrees. Therefore, extra time must be given for the cooking of many foods. The pretty lady from sea-level altitude should not be the least bit disgruntled about the "awful potatoes." They are possibly some of the finest "spuds" in the United States, grown in the famous potato district around Greeley, Colorado. Big red fellows, a large one, baked, is usually enough for two hungry people!

Of course, the Greeley resident could easily get into an argument with the farmer from Idaho who points to the big baked Idaho spud used by the Great Northern Railway. Both of them could come to blows with men from Montana, Utah, and in fact, any of the residents of the mountain states where dry, sandy soil produces big, mealy potatoes.

Thus it goes throughout the West from town to town and county seat to county seat. It may be a Mormon Ward Reunion in Utah or Southern Idaho; or a Basque gathering in Idaho or Nevada; or one of the big dairy picnics held in any state, where hundreds to thousands of people attend and bring their own lunches of fried chicken and baked beans and feast on the free ice cream and milk from the big creameries.

The Mormon gatherings are generally well-planned affairs under the supervision of the local bishop, who appoints committees on foods, entertainment, properties, and finance. Frequently the cooking is assigned to various women and carried out in the individual homes with the result that when grouped, there is a carefully planned menu. Sometimes it is a chance affair, called potluck; but most often it is planned. Occasionally the food is

cooked in a large central kitchen. Usually there are twenty to thirty different kinds of meats and vegetables served.

The Basques, although classified as a linguistic and social, rather than a
racial group, have kept many of their Spanish customs, which incidentally,
are not characteristic to all Spaniards, but only to Basques. Since coming to
America, and largely to the sagebrush country of Idaho, Nevada, and parts
of Montana and Wyoming, American customs have to an extent been blended into the Old Country traditions.

As most of the Basques follow the vocation of shepherding, their annual Sheepherder's Ball, where dress clothes are prohibited and denim overalls
are quite the thing, is of major importance. Usually the men wear bright
sashes, which lift their costumes from the commonplace to the colorful. In
December lamb and turkey auctions furnish an excuse for gaiety. Dancing,
singing, and feasting are indulged in at all times.

The famous chorizos, or sausages, of the Basques are made from pork cut
into small pieces, seasoned with salt, red pepper, a touch of garlic, and
preserved in shortening. Garbanzos, yellow beans about the size of a mid-
dle-sized pea, are a favorite. When boiled and properly seasoned, it becomes
larger than ordinary hominy and quite tasty. Huge cups of coffee, made half
with boiled milk and half with coffee, are drunk in prodigious amounts.
When liquor is added it becomes a coffee royal.

Hot dogs, beans, and beer, decidedly American, have become standard
for the annual Basque picnics in summer. In the holiday season, however,
from December 24 to January 6, the celebration goes to great lengths.
Christmas Eve is reserved for family reunions, but the remainder of the time
is spent in public dancing and feasting. January 6 is Three Kings Day, but in
America they do not exchange gifts on that day as is the case in the Old
Country, celebrating instead on Christmas in the American manner. A typical Basque dinner starts at eight o'clock in the evening and lasts four hours.

48

Lumber Camp Feed

ALL THROUGH THE ROCKY MOUNTAIN COUNTRY HUGE FORESTS OF WHITE PINE, DOUGLAS-FIR, CEDAR, AND SIMILAR TREES FURNISH MATERIAL FOR A LOGGING INDUSTRY THAT REACHES ITS PEAK IN WASHINGTON, OREGON, AND IDAHO. Here are hard-working men who require foods as robust as themselves, and the lumber camps have the reputation of furnishing the best that can be obtained.

In the old days a lumberjack had to content himself with such somber foods as sowbelly, beans, dried fruits, rice, corn meal, frozen beef, and the like. Today, that's all over with. No longer can it be said of the lumberjack:

When noon came round most anytime,
He grabbed a hunk of cheese,
A piece of tack,
From a gunny sack,
And made his old pipe wheeze.

When a logger goes after a job, he doesn't ask his prospective buddies if his tools will be sharp, or how the bunkhouse is laid out; all he asks is, "How do they feed?" That's the important thing in a logging camp and a jack, who will work all day in wet snow, doubled up in an uncomfortable position without saying a word, will cry his eyes out if his grub isn't up to what his family taste calls par.

The cook house is a huge building with a dining room off the kitchen that is capable of feeding three hundred or more workers at a meal. Rows of long wooden tables, glistening whitely from numerous lye scrubbings,

49

stretch lengthwise through the room. They are always set and ready for use with white porcelain or graniteware plates, cups and saucers, and the usual complement of knives, forks, and spoons.

It's an all-male establishment—cooks, flunkies, and loggers. Once, a story goes, a Puget Sound outfit hired a buxom Norwegian woman with flowing blonde tresses. They figured the feminine touch would be greatly appreciated; and it was, until the end of the first meal.

The woman was a real cook and had baked some pies that glowed with appetizing appearance. They were a golden brown with delicate little slashes

50

through which oozed a tempting juice, aromatically predicting a delicious treat to come. When the main course was finished a flunky proudly set the pie before the Bull of the Woods, who prepared for an enthusiastic onslaught. But before he had taken one bite, he pushed it disdainfully aside.

"What's the matter, Jiggers, don't you like pie?" queried one of the gang.

"Tell that cook to take it out and give it a shave and a haircut and I'll eat it," was the rejoinder.

Whether or not the story is true is immaterial, but women cooks are a rarity in the camps of the high timber country. And yet, these same men will fall all over themselves at a chance to eat a woman's cooking in a private home—a dish "like mother used to make" is their highest compliment at such times.

Few lumber camps serve a noon meal, it generally being eaten in the woods. But what breakfasts and what suppers! In the morning the clamor of the gut hammer, steel striking against steel, or the shrill notes of an electrically operated bell shatters the stillness of the woods and brings men boiling from the doors of the bunkhouses.

In front of each plate is a dish of fruit, usually canned prunes. These are generally ignored by the loggers and pushed aside. But in no time at all huge platters of fried bacon, eggs, potatoes, toast or biscuits, and hot cakes are on the table within easy reach of the jacks. From then on, it's every man for himself and no talk.

Conversation is confined to "Pass the grease" or "Wring that cow's tail and shove her this way," and the butter or milk is forwarded as per request. In the morning the men are dressed in "tin pants" and caulked boots on their way to the woods, but at night they wear soft pants and "henskin" shoes. Headgear is rarely removed, even for eating. No special table is set for company officials, the only recognition to their authority being the fact that their plates are set nearest the kitchen, separated from the men by an extra space, and that they are the only ones allowed to enter by way of the kitchen.

The evening meal is just as heavy with huge platters of roast beef and pork, carved from sizzling joints by the second cook and dishwasher; deep dishes of potatoes, peeled of their jackets; boiled onions; cabbage; tomatoes; and carrots. These are rushed to the tables by flunkies, one for every forty men, and it is an unpardonable sin to let a dish or platter become empty. Several kinds of desserts usually top off the meal.

In late April when the huge log drive down the north fork of the Clearwater River starts, cedar rafts are constructed, about seventy feet long and twenty feet wide. Canvas-covered frames are erected on these, one raft for the mess hall and the other for bunks. Here the loggers sleep and are fed. These odd structures are called "Wanigans."

The preference of the Scandinavian lumberjack to boiled food without too much seasoning is told by a cook who worked in a logging camp in western Montana. The cook was new and trying to please. He went to the trouble of cooking French doughnuts, Belgian baked potatoes, prime rib of beef (rare), buttered asparagus tips and corn muffins. He tried other things, but none of them seemed attractive to the men. One morning he changed the breakfast bill and served cottage-fried potatoes, southern-fried ham with natural sauce, and shirred eggs. When the meal was about half completed the superintendent came roaring into the kitchen:

> Gott Damnit to Hell, Kuuk, why in Hell don't you give us some-thing that's fit to eat. Everyday it's dem Gott Damned potatoes kuuked in fat. Don't you ever use water for anything but to mop the floor? Give us some potatoes wit de yakets on and some meat that's boiled—and burn that Gott Damn garlic. We want potatoes wit de yakets on, do you understand?

Livestock
Country Cooking

MALE COOKS LIKEWISE PREDOMINATE IN THE RANGE COUNTRY. HERE, A WOMAN IS ABOUT AS USEFUL AS AN ENGLISH POSTAGE-STAMP SADDLE; THEY'RE NOT MADE FOR ROUGH AND READY WORK. You could easily understand this if you ever saw an old range cook tearing across country in a chuck wagon, hell-bent for election, with the ends of his mustaches and the lines from his team streaming behind him like pennants in the breeze. They were great drivers and better cooks because they got there on time and weren't afraid to pick a new course if the occasion warranted it. The tradition has lasted.

The old-time range cook "got thar fustest" and had his camp set up and meal prepared by the time the cowboys drifted in for chuck. He carried everything in the wagon, including a pan of sourdough bread alongside of him on the seat, the jouncing of the wagon and an occasional poke with a flying elbow aiding in the kneading process.

The Dutch oven was the range cook's standby. He could fill it full of beans, put it in a bean hole covered by fire all night, and have the mess all done by morning. These, called in salty cowboy slang "whistleberries," were the range staple and served at almost every meal. Meat, because beef was cheap and available, was the other main item on the menu. In later days, dried fruits, beans, canned corn and tomatoes, occasionally sweet potatoes, flour, sugar, coffee, lard, and all kinds of seasoning were carried on the roundup. Eggs were served for a few days after the beef shipment, but they were too difficult to transport.

Eating utensils consisted mainly of tin cups and plates. At first there were few teaspoons, as they were too small to be of service to the trail hands and cowboys, who wolfed their food, rolled a smoke, and went back to work.

53

Later, teaspoons were common, and graniteware replaced to a large extent the tin plates and cups.

The mess, or chuck, wagon was fitted to accommodate the many accessories necessary on a roundup. It was usually covered with canvas and in the rear was the mess box with the cook's necessities and dishes. The lid of the box, when dropped onto a single-hinged leg, formed a table for the cook.

The regular meals were speedy affairs. A Wyoming doctor, who worked with the AUV outfit, tells of it:

By the time the drives were in there must have been upwards of eight thousand cattle on the roundup ground. On reaching camp it was remarkable how quickly the punchers hit the ground and unsaddled their horses. With equal alacrity the boys gulped down quarts of water, trying to quench their day-old thirst. No time was lost in filling our tin plates out of those Dutch ovens that were full of red-hot food. It was an unwritten law that this meal must be eaten in a hurry, as there were hungry and thirsty men holding the cattle who had a great desire to be relieved.

As quickly as a man finished eating, he grabbed his rope and caught his saddle horse, then away to herd, and what a joy to those punchers left with the herd to see him coming. In the shortest possible time those hungry and thirsty punchers were in camp putting away that meal, while other punchers were catching out their fresh horses and saddling them so that no time should be lost.

It would be after the herd was bedded and the campfire burning briskly, some puncher would slice an entire rib off the quarter of beef; leaving plenty of meat on it. Then he'd impale it on a stick of wood after he's hacked the meat. Now he would hold it over the hot coals and constantly twirl it. When it was roasted, pepper and salt were added, then what a delicious feed one could have.

54

Even though the cowboy was forced to live on rough and ready food, mostly of the dried variety, it didn't stifle his craving for green vegetables and fresh foods. Many is the cowpuncher who worked for less wages at certain smaller ranches, just because they had a garden and served varied food. Emerson Hough says:

> The cowboy thinks of fresh vegetables in his epicurean dreams, and he longs for the indigestible pies of civilization. Any cowpuncher would sell his birthright for half a dozen pies. The cow cook cannot make actual pies, only leathery imitations encasing stewed dried apples. One remembers very well a certain Christmas dinner in a little far-away Western plains town which cost two men twenty-five dollars, and which consisted of some badly cooked beef, one can of oysters, a frosted cake, and five green onions, the latter obtained from somewhere by a hothouse miracle. This dinner was voted a very extraordinary and successful affair.

Fresh eggs also were a greatly desired luxury. John J. (Sarge) Caldwell, former N-N cowboy, tells how his craving for eggs, bolstered with courage from a bottle of whiskey, caused him to order four dozen soft-boiled eggs one day when he was in town. And he ate just about all of them, at that.

Of course, all this is over with, now. The range cooks with their galloping teams are a thing of the past. They come out with their chuck wagons only when the Stockmens Association, the Range Riders Association, or some cow town is putting on a roundup revival of the old days or a rodeo. Gone, too, is the lonely ranchwoman and her poignant story of searching the supplies hauled in by the men for fresh fruit and meat and finding only dried fruit and sowbelly so that "she cried and cried until it seemed as if she would never stop." They are all gone, but their heritage lingers into the present.

55

Throughout the West is the imprint of the old range cook. The things he accomplished under the spur of necessity have been made easier through modern advances and today offer taste sensations that have withstood the test of time. They are preserved in the ranch homes and featured in the romantic atmosphere of the dude ranches. Furthermore, they are godsends to the packer, hunter, fisherman, and Western outdoor man, who must face temporarily the problems of cooking that were everyday occurrences to the old-time cook.

Take son-of-a-bitch in a sack, for instance. That's what they called it before dainty lady dudes in jodhpurs made their appearance. Today, it's somewhat shamefacedly referred to as son-of-a-gun. Nevertheless, despite the change in name, it hasn't lost any of its old-time attraction. It's like the story J. Frank Dobie tells of the cow horse that was named Old Guts in the typically salty and descriptive manner of the cowboy. It seems that he had an internal structure that caused his entrails to rumble and churn when he struck a rough gait. This day, the cowboy was out riding with a particularly insistent governess. She wanted to know the horse's name and the cowboy wanted to change the subject. As usual, the woman won out, but the cowboy softened it up somewhat with characteristic chivalry. He told her the horse was named Old Bowels, but the horse rumbled on just the same. That's the way it is with son-of-a-gun in a sack and its more substantial companion, son-of-a-gun stew.

For son-of-a-gun in a sack you take water, flour, sugar, salt, and baking powder and make a soft dough. Then you add raisins, dried apples, and suet. In the old days this mass was placed in a sack with space enough for the apples to swell and dropped in a kettle of boiling water to cook for several hours. Today, it is merely steamed in a steamer. Either way, it's all the same, and when served with a sweet sauce made of water thickened with flour and sweetened with sugar plus a little cinnamon for flavor, it's quite a treat.

Son-of-a-gun stew is a bit more complicated. This treat comes the evening a beef is butchered. You slice up a good supply of the leaf fat that is found around the stomach and place it in a Dutch oven. About fifteen slices of liver, a half-inch thick, are added, along with the sweetbread found near the large intestine. Then, the smallest intestine, which is always empty and is called the marrowgut, is sliced into pieces about three inches in length. The kidneys and the butcher steak are then sliced and added. The butcher steak is the thick part of the diaphragm where it fastens to the back. Salt and pepper is added and it is all stirred together until nicely browned in the hot fat. When the lid comes off, a rich odor is released that is a combination of clear fresh fat mingled with the delicate odor of fried meat.

The beauty of the roundup cook's talents is that it reaches its peak in camp cookery and there's nothing the true Westerner likes better than to get out-of-doors. The smell of wood smoke and sage in the clear mountain air, mingling with the seductive smells of frying, broiling, and roasting food, teases the appetite into frenzied hunger. And above all, despite feminine ingression, the outdoors still is a man's world.

The average woman who spends her time digging into "the corners" and ferreting out "the little things of life" is more or less lost in the vastness of the plains country and in the grandeur of the mountains; she can't get along without "the little things." Take the matter of bread. A Western packer swings down from his horse by a mountain steam or lake and starts to pitch camp. The fire is started; a tin pail is emptied of salt, pepper, baking powder, matches, and similar small articles; then, filled with water, it is put on the fire to boil for coffee. The sack of flour is placed nearby and the packer is ready to start making bread.

Of course, there's no table. There's no mixing pan, either. None is needed. The sack of flour is opened and inside is a little ball of dough—the starter. A depression is patted into the flour in the sack and water is poured into the hole. The starter is left there to soak, while the packer slices bacon into a skillet and puts it on to fry.

While the bacon is frying, potatoes and onions are peeled. By this time the bacon is done. It is put on a plate near the fire and most of the grease is poured off, either into a cup or onto the plate with the bacon. Then, back to the bread. Salt, baking powder, a little flour scooped down from the sides of the depression, and there is a large wad of dough. It's spread over the frying pan—not all the dough; you have to save some for the next starter. That's rolled into a stiff ball and left in the flour sack.

When the frying bread is brown on one side, it's turned over. Meanwhile the potatoes and onions are being diced. When the bread is browned on the other side and firm clear through, it's lifted out of the frying pan and stood on edge against a rock alongside the fire to continue cooking.

Back into the frying pan goes the bacon grease that was poured off. Then the diced potatoes and onion are added. By now, things are getting tough. The pungent odor of fried bacon, bolstered by the delicious smell of hot fried bread, is teasing the tastebuds of the packer and whipping up his appetite. But he adds to his own misery. He dumps a handful of coffee into the pail of boiling water and adds a new aggravating foreign smell to accentuate his hunger. By this time the stronger smell of frying onions is forcing its way through the coffee odor and the packer gives the mixture of potatoes and onions a stir. Water is added; a lid is put on the skillet, and the onions and potatoes left to steam soft.

If the packer has a steak along, whether elk or beef, now's the time to cook it, because he'll like it rare. A green stick is shoved through at each end and the stick is twirled over the fire until the steak is done. Salt and pepper, and what a feed! All told it didn't take more than half an hour. And the delicious outdoor smells, mingled with those of the sizzling hot food, are not marred by the thought of stacks of dishes to wash. A cigarette, a tree for a back rest, and the Devil takes his troubles.

But this isn't the only thing that can be done in camp. This is just a quickie. Take the large trout found in Jackson Lake, Wyoming, or in hundreds of other mountain lakes from Wyoming to California. Try baking it inside a buttered Dutch oven or over a grill of green pole wood. But remember to baste it continually with a mixture of butter, vinegar, mustard, salt, and pepper.

There's plenty of wild game in this vast Western country—antelope, deer, elk, mountain goats, duck, geese, grouse, pheasants, partridges, and lots more. And when it's cooked right, there's nothing can beat it. Oftentimes, sportsmen commit the blunder of placing small game into the skillet without giving it time to cool. The result is that it is tough, stringy, and tasteless. All small game, both feathered and furred, should hang for at least several hours before using; several days is better.

Small game is delicious broiled or roasted on a skewer. Slices of salt pork, pinned to the sides with slivers of wood, add much to the flavor and keep the meat from drying.

Large game animals should be allowed to ripen for a week or so before using. The saddle and shoulder are the best cuts for roasting and these may be barbecued in the regular way. Steaks are broiled or fried. But, regardless of the method used, there's something about wild game, with its rich, heady aroma and sharp, off-trail flavor that makes it the only real food for the camp menu.

Mulligans are popular throughout the West, to say nothing of what one old-timer calls a "homogeneous mass." The homogeneous mass differs from the mulligan, which is usually composed of beef, potatoes, onions, and sometimes cabbage, plus an occasional vegetable, in that it is frankly a "house cleaning." All the leftovers are dumped into a kettle along with meat and cooked into a stew that is never the same at each repetition. Regardless of content, the mulligan has an element of surprise and an aroma to stimulate the most timid of tastes.

Biscuits are usually served with almost everything and vie with hot cakes in popularity. Dutch oven biscuits, eaten out-of-doors, have a taste all their own, even though they are made in the conventional manner. Buttering the outside so they won't stick to the oven seems to "do something" to them.

This outdoor cookery is so popular that thousands of tourists as well as natives spend a large portion of their recreation hours in the forests and along streams and lakes in an effort to recapture the life of the old-time cowboy. Nevertheless, it isn't all for the sake of fun. The Western sheepherder has varied his way of life to a very small degree since the days of the open range. Unlike the cowboy, he continues to live the same old life.

A sheepherder's existence is almost always a lonely one. He must stay with his band of sheep, and his only chance for a splurge is when he makes his rare visits to town and tries to gorge himself with whiskey, oysters, and eggs to last through another long session with the woolies. He's like the prospector and the old-time cowboy when he goes to town. He wants to do it all at once, but he just hasn't the time and he doesn't know how. Nevertheless, his life at his sheep wagon is still of the Old West. But let Archer B. Gilfillan of South Dakota tell about it:

The average person might think that the bill of fare on a sheep ranch would show a preponderance of mutton and lamb, as far as the meat course is concerned. Strange to say, just the opposite is true. The sheepman raises mutton, but he almost never eats it, and neither does the herder. As far as lamb is concerned, the sheepman feels that he cannot afford it. To eat a ewe lamb would be to deprive himself of a long line of the lamb's possible descendants, while to eat a wether or male lamb would be dipping into one of his two cash crops a year— lambs and wool.

To this is added the difficulty of keeping fresh meat in any quantity during the summer months in the sparse ranching region, where the only form of refrigeration is a small icebox supplied with ice cut from some adjacent pond and stored in a dugout. Therefore, the rancher is apt to butcher a young steer or fat cow as soon as cold weather comes to act as a preservative and to put down a large hog or two early in the spring for the summer's meat.

On the average sheep ranch, mutton will be eaten only about twice a year. Once during the winter some large wether that was missed at shipping time will be butchered to vary the monotony of the beef diet. The wether, while heavier than the wether lamb, is not worth as much per pound and is of course productive of nothing but wool. The only time of the year when a mutton is sure to be butchered is shearing time. With the shearing crew and the extra helpers to be fed, it is possible to dispose of an entire sheep carcass even during comparatively warm weather.

As to the herder's diet, it depends largely on the boss's own ideas on the subject. Obviously the herder, living in his sheep wagon, cannot eat what the boss does not bring him. This is illustrated by the story of the sheepman who brought his herder a sack of flour, a can of coffee, and a slab of salt pork and told him to cook anything he wanted.

Owing to the absolute lack of refrigeration, the sheepherder's meat is largely confined to ham, bacon, and eggs during the summer months. This may be supplemented by such young jacks and cottontails as he may be able to shoot, or by an occasional taste of lamb or mutton, when some coyote has done a thorough job of butchering and bleeding the victim before being discovered. One bunch of sheep at shipping time was found to be short several of its early fat

62

lambs and the herder was never able to convince his boss that they
had been stolen from him by a neighboring herder at night. Perhaps
one should say his ex-boss.

A typical meal in a sheep wagon would be ham or bacon, fried
potatoes, a canned vegetable of some kind—either beans, peas, or
tomatoes—bread and butter, and coffee. Sometimes there will be
stewed apricots or apples for dessert with perhaps a sprinkling of
raisins. Sheep wagon fare is plain, substantial, and devoid of any frills.
Since the herder lives alone, there is never any complaint about the
cooking.

While this meal seems ordinary enough, it is prepared under most

63

unusual conditions. The sheep wagon, with its strictly limited space, is a model of compactness. The stove, the dish cupboard above it, and the table hinged to the bunk in the rear are all within reaching distance of the small open space near the front of the wagon. Hence the herder is able to get a meal, eat it, and then wash the dishes without, literally, stirring out of his tracks.

The sheep wagon is situated anywhere from one to six miles from the buildings of the ranch to which it is attached, and the ranch itself is frequently far from any highway. It might seem, therefore, that the herder would be a very lonesome individual, rarely seeing anyone. Such is not the case, however, for in a range country, unfenced for the most part, stock is continually straying and men are continuously riding after it. All these riders are likely to approach the sheepherder, if they see him, because he is the one most apt to know whether the missing stock is in that region. And if it is near mealtime, the hospitable herder will invite the rider to eat. He is glad to do so, because he knows that the rider will repay the favor by telling him of any sheep that may chance to stray away.

Once in a while two sheep wagons will be close enough together for the herders to entertain one another, and on such occasions they put their best foot forward, and the most prized can is opened. Each knows that he can get back at the other for any hospitality extended and each wishes to display his culinary skill before a fellow craftsman.

The rider for stock and the neighboring sheepherder are both welcome to a meal at the wagon, but there is a third class, most numerous of all, that tries the herder's patience and half convinces him that he is playing the role of an unpaid hotel keeper. This is the bachelor, homesteader, or small farmer whose land adjoins the sheep range at the point where the wagon stands at the time. With regard to him, the sheepherder is in a peculiar position. He does not dare offend him, because his sheep are likely to stray across the line at any time, and it pays him to be on the friendliest terms with the owner of the land while offering one of the numerous alibis that the herder always keeps on hand for emergencies. But when that neighbor develops the habit of dropping in just about mealtime, the herder begins to harbor the suspicion that the neighbor is not so much attracted by the charm of his conversation as he is revolted by the thought of having to get his own dinner, and this in turn induces a revulsion in the mind of the herder, to the point of wishing that he could slip a little prussic acid into the coffee, except for the danger of getting some of it himself.

If the wagon happens to be situated near a highway, the herder will have still another kind of visitor—the tourist. The man from the East or South is apt to be curious about this home on wheels with the smoke coming out of the stovepipe. His curiosity seldom is strong enough to lead him to accept an invitation to dinner, perhaps through a natural distrust of the sanitary arrangements. But the one question he is simply bound to ask is, how many sheep are there in the bunch? This is embarrassing for the herder, because this is information that he is not supposed to divulge, for the reason that the numbers on the statement to the bank and the statement of the assessor do not always agree.

When sheepmen foregather in convention, they are apt to break through their inhibitions and have mutton for their banquet dish, after which they get up and make long speeches to one another about how to get other people—except sheepmen—to eat more lamb. A lamb growers' association near Newell, South Dakota, has barbecued lamb as the feature of its yearly meeting and banquet. Yet it may still be said that the sheepman and the herder don't eat mutton—they grow it.

Once every year in the livestock country comes a gustatory treat that makes what the cowboys call "laurpin good truck." This occurs in the spring during, if it's on a sheep ranch, docking time, or, if it's on a cattle ranch, branding time. Docking time or branding time, it's all the same—it's the time when the famous Rocky Mountain or prairie oyster is in season.

When the lambs are gathered for marking and their tails are docked, or cut off, the male lambs are castrated. A similar event takes place on the cattle ranch when the calves are branded. The testicles comprise the Rocky Mountain oyster. Here, the cattleman has it on the sheepman, as his oyster is a more sizable product; hence, we'll describe the scene at the cattle ranch.

The two men doing the branding are the official chefs. A chunk of tin or a clean flat rock is placed at one end of the branding fire to serve as a grill. Nearby is a large bucket of water and a sack partially filled with flour, salt, and pepper. As the calves are castrated the testicles are tossed into the pail of water for cleaning. From time to time, as a lull comes in the work, the testicles or oysters are fished out, dropped into the sack, and shaken around so that they speedily become flour coated and seasoned. Then they are placed on the grill to cook.

Despite the nauseating smell of burned hair from the branding, it is claimed that cowboys holding the herd at some distance away from the fire can tell by the odor of the fries the precise moment when they are done. Whether or not it is true, they are Johnny-on-the-spot for their share of the delicacy. As one old cowman expressed it, "It may have been my youth or the long hours we worked, from sunup to sunset, which caused me to be continually hungry; but in between meals—Man! Oh, man!—were those calf fries good!"

In the more mountainous sections of the West where the roundups are smaller and consequently less work, the oysters are saved until the branding is finished and toasted on the end of a stick over fire. Sometimes the feast takes place indoors. Here, like in the branding corral, it is strictly a male affair. A Montana ranchwoman gives the woman's viewpoint as follows:

> I am ignorant as to the preparation, even to the serving. There comes a call, "All women out of the kitchen, a couple of cowhands are taking over." We vanish. I know all the skillets in the house are used and plenty of butter. Rolled cracker crumbs are also in evidence. From the kitchen comes a delicious odor—something like real oysters out of season. Lots of gaiety. It must be fun.

Barbecue Blowouts

AS A RESULT OF THIS TRADITION OF MASCULINE COOKERY, A MAN WHO DONS AN APRON AND ENTERS A KITCHEN OR APPROACHES AN OUTDOOR FIRE IS NOT LOOKED UPON WITH SCORN IN THE WEST. Instead, the sight conjures visions of robust food, savory, and with aroma lusty enough to banish all such anemic things as lettuce sandwiches and frail tidbits. That's why barbecues are popular and men like Buck Lee of Utah, the "best damned artist" in the San Juan, are respected.

Buck is known for his tall tales and "desert broiled" steaks. Buck's steak is no dainty mignon; it is a healthy slab two to three inches thick. When he smears one with lard, salt, and pepper, and lays it across grills placed four inches above a bed of hot coals, you have time to savor the thing with your nostrils. You can inhale the goodness of it as it sizzles and pops. And you have time to do it, too. There's time enough for the aroma to stimulate your gastric juices and get you ready for the goodness to come. And when the steak is done, with its flavor like old scotch ripened above peat smoke on a Highland moor, you wonder if the "best damned artist" in the San Juan can paint, too.

Of course, these are intimate little affairs, even though an agoraphobic might dispute the fact. They are intimate to a Westerner who considers any gathering of a dozen or fewer persons intimate and a background of sentinel-like mountains towering above a forest of purple-green pines as downright cozy. But for your big blowouts, they'll take a barbecue everytime.

At a smaller barbecue it is not unusual to take the head and shoulders of a beef, unskinned, and place it in a pit that has been lined with live coals. The beef is then covered with coals, and dirt is shoveled in to retain every bit of heat. The next morning when the meat is disinterred, it is tender and full of flavor. Of course, even if such an affair is called small, it should be remembered that the head and shoulders of beef will feed several persons.

At the big affairs, a huge trench is dug and wood is burned until a deep layer of coals is accumulated. A whole beef is skinned and chained to a crossbar or broken and spread over a grill sometimes made of steel rails. Occasionally the whole beef is buried unskinned right in the pit. Frequently, however, the beef is butchered and quantities of meat are suspended from a green cross-log above the open pit. When the meat is skinned and roasted in the open, it is swabbed from time to time with a mixture of tallow, water, salt, and pepper.

The cooking is started the day before the gathering is to take place, in some shaded grove or along a mountain stream generally referred to locally as "the picnic grounds." Ranchers and townspeople start gathering early, sniffing the air and critically watching the progress of the cooks. Practically all bring flasks, and the bottle is passed around to be drunk straight with no chaser. Tables are piled high with buns, pickles, apples, and similar items. Coffee is served piping hot in tin cups. The meat has been donated by various ranchers, and other food, by businessmen in the "trading center."

As a rule there is no "program," the day being spent in visiting. However, if the affair marks a national or local holiday, or if it comes before an election, some speeches are made. Nevertheless, visiting and eating are most important.

E. W. Runge, an old-time barbecue cook, insists that the sealed pit method is the best:

> The meat is cut in pieces and wrapped in clean burlap. It is not seasoned, as seasoning causes the juice to run out. We put the meat in the pit right on the coals, covered the pit with a pieces of sheet iron, heaped sand over it and let the meat cook. I do not like the spit method as the meat is charred and not well done. There is too much waste, as too much has to be thrown away. The same with the grill method. I have helped at many barbecues, and experience taught me that the sealed-pit method is the best.

Tom Gregory, another old-time cowboy, describes a barbecue in which the spit method is used:

> At the end of the roundup season, the stockman-owner would have several head of prime beef slaughtered. Several large rectangular holes, or "spits," were dug by the cowboys to be used by the ranch cooks for roasting the beeves. The beeves were never cut up for cooking during the barbecue, but were securely fastened to heavy, slender, green poles, fixed with handles and wedged in thick, forked

69

poles driven into the ground at each end of the spit. A hot, roaring fire was kindled in the bottom of the spit and the beeves were turned over and over the fire to assure a nice brown to the meat. Man, you could smell that odor for miles around, and it made your mouth water to smell it! Those ranch cooks sure knew how to do their stuff, and when you saw the juicy meat, with the juice dripping from it, you could hardly wait till it was done. But meat was not all there was to eat. There were loads and loads of boiled and mashed potatoes, steaming hot; there were bowls and bowls of juicy brown gravy; your choice of brown or white homemade bread; string beans; pickled beets; peas in cream; apple sauce; mustard and horse radish; hot coffee and tea; milk and cold spring water. Well, it was enough to test the appetite of anyone who happened to be around. Nothing was ever allowed to get cold, except at night, when everybody had had their fill during the day and were willing to just sit around and be lazy until time to go to bed. Even then the delicious smell of the food was good.

Besides furnishing their own meat, the stockmen always purchased the other eats and drink for the barbecues they put on. A wagon was sent to town and the driver had instructions to purchase large quantities of these vegetables and staple foods and charge them to the stockman. Upon arriving back at the home ranch, all cowboys went to work, shelling peas, cutting up beans, and peeling potatoes for the feast which was to take place the following day. All of them would do their duties although they didn't like it very much. They didn't like to do anything, anyhow, that they couldn't do while riding a horse; but as long as they were told to do things by the boss, they would do them. Then after these chores were done, they had to go out and fell trees, cut them up, and split them into firewood to be

71

used for the cooking of the barbecue feed. After all the chores were done, they had it easy because the camp cooks would do all the rest of the work and they could eat and mix with the crowd and really enjoy themselves during the barbecue.

Whenever one of these barbecues were to be held, notices were posted up in towns and where anyone could see them. These notices would tell when the feast would start and where they were to be held. It would show "FREE ADMISSION" in big letters with a request for all those attending to bring their own plates and cups and silverware. No tables were ever set for a barbecue feast and all food was served, piping hot, from the big kettles and the meat cut in large slices from the hot, roasted beef. Everyone attending the barbecue would form a long line and proceed from one kettle to the next, where a cook would give each one a large serving of every kind of food and drink they wanted. Then with their plates heaping full, everyone would go and sit on the ground or on blankets, if they thought to bring any along with them. Some tried to make pigs of themselves and go back for seconds and thirds and then found them-selves with severe stomachaches, but you were welcome to eat all you wanted, anytime you wanted it, until the feast was over. When the feasts were finally over, there was nothing left of any kind of food. Everyone had had all he could eat and some had had much more than they could eat; but everyone had been satisfied, and all had had a wonderful time and a grand outdoor feed. At the end of the bar-becue, all attending would thank the stockman who had made the barbecue possible, the cooks and those who had helped to put it over. Then taking their leaves, they would head for home.

Thousands of persons are sometimes served at one barbecue and a "master of the barbecue" gains more than a local reputation. The Texas influence was strong in Wyoming and Montana, where Texas cattlemen brought their customs to the northern ranges. This influence is also evident in the small towns and villages of the cattle country to the east, but varies in sections according to the influence of other peoples, both foreign and American.

Here, too, in the cattle country, the wealthy ranchers, like the wealthy mining men, molded customs to some extent. Cheyenne, Wyoming, like Miles City, Montana, had its clubs and hotels where elaborate menus were served. Also, some of the old range cooks like George Bickler of the UL Ranch acquired reputations for elaborate dinners that gave them the same prestige among the cattlemen that Eastern chefs, such as Oscar at the Waldorf, enjoyed among the haut monde. One time Bickler featured at a UL dinner a range cow carved from a block of ice with a hot poker as a centerpiece. The back was hollowed out for a nest of raw oysters, brought especially from Baltimore, Maryland. Roast pork, however, was the cattleman's symbol of luxury, pork being a rarity on the range. For this reason ham and eggs and fried potatoes is one of the delicacies of the West. After living on salt pork or bacon and beans, fresh eggs and real ham grew to mean something special.

Conclusion

TODAY THE EATING AND DRINKING HABITS OF THE WEST, LIKE THE PEOPLE THEMSELVES, ARE A BLEND OF EUROPE AND AMERICA, THE OLD WEST AND OLDER EAST. At the base remains the old stock, northern European influence, always present to some degree, and the original recipes and food habits by the pioneer emigrants who came in by sailboat, by horse, and by oxen from New England and the

73

South, then the Middle West. These habits were modified by the necessity of a harder life on the sagebrush plains and the shining mountains, from the previous experiences of the fur traders and trappers, the mountain men and their antecedents, the Indian scouts, buffalo hunters, cowboys, miners, and lumberjacks. Then came a blending of the older stock, northern European and American homespun, with the later homesteaders and sheepmen, the merchants and professional people, the dry-land and irrigation farmers, construction crews, fisher folk, industrialists and their laborers. Into all this came the habits of the newer immigrants, the Ellis Island, Italians and Russians, Serbs and Syrians, Basque, Czech, and "Bohunk." As the boom mining camps metamorphosed into industrial centers, vast ranch empires into modern agricultural centers, and timber domains into populated residential areas, so metamorphosed and were molded the present-day foodstuffs and eating habits.

A westerner today is still, by and large, a rugged, physical specimen, an independent, democratic, jovial individual given to excesses—generous, boisterous, vigorous. So then, are his foods, and his eating and drinking habits. Whether on the table of the city banker or the dry-land farmer, Western food is substantial, always. It may have the frills of a French chef's influence or of a home economist's college dietetics training; but, nevertheless, the staple items of the farm and the range, the mining camp boarding house, and the lumberjacks' mess hall predominate today.

Recipe Appendix:
Statewide Specialities

COLORADO

Mock Baked Potatoes

Since baking takes a long time—and lots of firewood—potatoes are frequently boiled in water in which 6, 7, or 8 tablespoons of salt (rock salt, if available) have been dissolved. The increased heat of the boiling water due to the presence of the salt cooks the potatoes as if they have been baked except that the skins are thinner. If placed in a hot oven for 2 or 3 minutes, they cannot be distinguished from true baked potatoes.

India Pickle (Not to be confused with India Relish)

The product of this recipe may be used to make Thousand Island Dressing, as the filler for Spanish omelets, as a sandwich spread, as a sauce for meat loaves, or in the loaf itself. It is also good with baked beans. Place 12 apples, 10 ripe tomatoes, 9 medium onions, and 3 cups vinegar in a kettle. When this comes to a boil, add 3 cups sugar, 1/4 cup salt, 1/2 teaspoon cinnamon, 1/8 teaspoon cloves, and 1/2 teaspoon black pepper. Cook until tender and seal.

Roast Venison

Rub a leg or saddle of venison with butter, wrap it in buttered paper, and place it in a roasting pan. Make a thick paste of flour and water, and apply a half-inch coating of this to the paper. Put a pint of water in pan, cover the latter, and roast in a moderately slow oven, allowing 30 minutes of roasting time for each pound of meat and basting every 15 minutes after the first

75

hour. Before serving, remove paper wrapping and baste with a sauce of melted butter, flour, salt, and pepper.

Smoked Trout

A delicacy not to be found on any restaurant menu is smoked native or brook trout. Preparation of this chef-d'oeuvre assumes an ample supply (from 50 to 200 pounds) of freshly caught trout, since the time and labor required in the operations would not warrant dealing with a picayune quantity. The place of preparation should be in the mountains where plenty of the right variety of willow for smoking may be secured—almost any lake will do. The next step is to build a conical tepee or wickiup of stout green boughs covered with leaves. Then, from the nearby marshes or shores of the lake, loads of young willows are brought by canoe to the improvised smokehouse. When the fish have been suspended inside the structure, a subdued, smoky fire of willow twigs is maintained for 24 hours—a task requiring energy, patience, and an optimism that is justified by the results. After the smoked trout are dressed with butter in a hot pan and cooked over the glowing camp coals, the gourmand has only to take the final step and eat as heartily as he likes, while the rest of the catch can be conveniently shipped from the mountains to his home.

IDAHO

Honey Gingerbread

Sift 1/2 teaspoon cinnamon, 1/2 teaspoon cloves, 1/2 teaspoon ginger, and 1/2 teaspoon salt with 1 cup Idaho beet sugar. Beat 3 eggs into this. Add 1 cup strained honey and 1 cup sour cream, beating. Add 4 cups flour and 2 teaspoons soda sifted together. The mixture will be quite stiff. Bake in well-greased pans in moderate oven. Delicious hot or cold.

Baked Hash

Grind up leftover meat. Chop cold, cooked potatoes. Combine two parts potato to one part meat. Add some chopped onion to taste and plenty of salt, pepper, and butter. Add less butter if meat has some fat. Add enough hot water to simmer slowly in a baking pan in the oven for a good hour. An iron pan is best. The hash should brown down toward the last but will not dry out entirely if not cooked in too hot an oven.

Baked Onions

Remove center of onion, fill with breadcrumbs, cheese, and seasoning, including ginger.

Baked Beans

In the high altitude of the hills or mountain slopes it requires much time to cook beans when boiled over an open fire, so the camp cook would wash the navy beans, put them in the Dutch oven, and bring them to a brisk boil over the open fire, adding bacon, salt, and pepper. Then the cook would dig a hole in the earth, line it with hot coals, and place the oven in the pit. The top was then covered with coals and dirt shoveled in to retain the heat. In the morning the beans were cooked to a "queen's taste."

MONTANA

Ragout of Lamb

Needed: 2 pounds shoulder lamb, 2 teaspoons salt, 2 minced onions, 1 large can tomatoes, 1 cup water, 1/2 can peas, flour, bacon fat.

Brown the lamb in the bacon fat. (Lamb should be cut in small pieces.) Add tomatoes and bring to a boil, then add onions and brown. Add water, put all in a casserole or stewing dish, cook slowly for 2 hours, replenishing the water as it boils away.

Corned Beef and Cabbage

Let a piece (4 or 5 pounds) of corned beef soak for an hour in cold water, drain it, and place in fresh, boiling water in a large kettle. Cook 5 hours until tender; 20 minutes before finished add cabbage. Turnips and carrots sometimes are used. Serve with boiled potatoes.

Ham and Eggs and Fried Spuds

Take center slices of ham; trim excess fat. Place excess fat in skillet to form grease in which ham slices are fried. Fry ham slices slowly so that they will not become hard and tough. Remove ham to platter and break eggs into skillet. By placing a top over the skillet, a white covering forms over the eggs, which some people like better than "sunny-side up." This is a matter of choice. Meanwhile in another skillet in which ham grease and butter have been placed, boiled potatoes are sliced and fried brown. If the potatoes have not been previously boiled, a small amount of water should be placed in the skillet, which is covered with a top so the potatoes may steam. Variations to this may include the adding of sliced onions to the frying potatoes. A raw egg also may be broken into the potatoes when they are done, and all stirred together as another variation.

Pasty

Roll out a pie crust, not too rich. Cut in pieces 10 by 16 inches. Cut up several large potatoes. Use half as much lean beef cut in small pieces as potatoes. Add 1 good-sized onion. A good-sized piece of butter is mixed with this filling. Season to taste. Fill one half of each cut piece of dough, fold over, and press edges firmly together. Dent pasties with fork. Place in medium oven and bake until done. One uses as much of the potato and meat mixture as there are pieces of dough rolled out to fill them.

Venison Mincemeat

Venison meat is often used in mincemeat pies in this region. Venison is substituted for beef in a regular mincemeat recipe. Other types of wild game are often used as well.

NEVADA

Sourdough

The following recipe for sourdough is the old, original style, as used by the old-timers of early days. To 1 quart of lukewarm water add a teacupful of sugar and enough flour to make a batter as for pancakes. Set it in a warm place until fermentation sets in, which will take from 1 to 3 days, depending upon temperature, and will be ready to use when bubbles form throughout the mass. In mixing, use an earthen, glass, or wooden receptacle, or an unchipped granite-coated one.

Sourdough Bread

To make sourdough bread add to the sourdough 2 teaspoonfuls of salt, 2 tablespoonfuls of lard or butter, 2 quarts of flour, and enough warm water to make into a stiff dough. Mix thoroughly and knead from 5 to 10 minutes. Set aside in a warm place and let rise until it doubles in size. Again knead, lightly, and mold into loaves. Place into greased bread pans and let rise again until once more it doubles in size. Then bake in a moderate oven from 45 minutes to 1 hour.

Sourdough Biscuits

Mix 1 pint of flour and 1 teaspoon of salt with 1 pint of warm water or canned milk. Beat into a smooth batter and keep in a warm place until well soured or fermented; then add another teaspoon of salt, 1 1/2 teaspoons of soda dissolved in 1/2 cup of tepid water, and enough flour to make the dough easy to handle. Knead thoroughly until dough is no longer sticky, then cut up into biscuits and cook in a pan containing plenty of grease.

Pancakes

Sourdough pancakes are still to many families of the West what the buck-wheat cakes and corn cakes are to those of the East and South. After adding soda to the sourdough, as for biscuits, thin to a batter with milk and add 1 or 2 eggs, then fry as any pancake is fried.

Suet Pudding

The roundup cook took great pride in his pies, although he had only stewed, dried fruit from which to make them. But, his greatest triumph was, perhaps, the suet pudding. The pies were placed in ordinary, tin pie plates and baked in the Dutch oven, which was first heated well. With a low fire of coals beneath and coals and ashes over the top, a pie would bake and brown in a short time and the process could be repeated until the required number was ready for the hungry crew.

The suet pudding was more of a rarity, although suet was naturally plentiful where beef was so frequently butchered. It was made as follows: 1 cup of chopped suet, 1/2 teaspoon of salt, 2 teaspoons of baking powder, and 1/2 cup of breadcrumbs. These ingredients were mixed into a stiff dough with 2 cups of water. The dough was then rolled in flour and placed in a bag, leaving room to "swell." It was then placed in boiling water in the Dutch oven, covered, and boiled over the campfire for 2 hours. Served with a plain sauce

80

of water and sugar, thickened with a little flour and with a teaspoon of vanilla or other extract for flavoring, it was a welcome change from the usual camp fare.

Broiling Steaks

Broiled steaks are, there is no doubt of it, much more palatable than fried. Broiling retains the juices and imparts a delicious flavor. To broil, cut the steak from 1 inch to 1 1/2 inches thick. Season with salt and pepper if desired, clamp it between the broiler grids and place over glowing coals, or prop it before the fire. Adjust distance so steak will be done in center without having the outside burned. Turn frequently. Serve hot with butter, or with gravy made from the drippings caught in a pan.

OREGON

Huckleberry Griddle Cakes

Sift together 2 cups of flour, 1 teaspoon of salt, and 1 1/2 teaspoons of baking powder. Combine with 1 beaten egg, 1 1/2 cups of sour milk, and 1 teaspoon of soda. Then add 1 teaspoon of melted butter and 1 cup of huckleberries. Bake on hot, greased griddle, and serve with syrup of thick huckleberry sauce.

McGinties

Wash 1 pound of dried apples, removing bits of core and skin, and soak overnight. Next day stew in enough water to cover, and when soft run through a colander. Replace on stove, add enough brown sugar to make the fruit rich and sweet, and cook until thick; then cool and add 1 1/2 tablespoons of ground cinnamon. Line a dripping-pan with pie crust, put in fruit mixture, and cover with upper crust, gashing the latter slightly to let the steam escape. Press edges of crust together and bake—at first in a hot oven, then reducing the heat. When done, cut into diamond-shaped portions and serve hot with cream.

Smelt
Heat 2 tablespoons of olive oil or bacon grease in a skillet and brown therein a small quantity of minced onions, garlic, and green pepper. Add a can of tomato sauce and let simmer for 5 minutes; then add 1/2 cup vinegar and cook 2 minutes longer. Meanwhile dredge the smelt in flour and fry until brown and tender. Place fish on a platter and pour the sauce over it.

Cheese Sauce for Boiled fish
Melt 2 tablespoons of butter in the top of a double boiler and add 1 1/2 tablespoons of flour, 1/2 teaspoon of salt, and 1/4 teaspoon of pepper and paprika. Blend thoroughly and add gradually 1 1/2 cups of milk. Cook for 10 minutes, stirring constantly, then add 1/2 pound of cheese grated or cut into small pieces, and beat with an eggbeater until the cheese is melted. After draining the fish, pour the sauce over it and garnish with parsley and lemon.

UTAH

Brown Cake
Prepare everything before beginning cake. Shave and melt squares of Baker's unsweetened chocolate over hot water. Sift 1 cup flour. Add 2 teaspoons baking powder to another 3/4 cup sifted flour and sift. Butter pan. Shell and chop 1 cup English walnuts. Cream 3/4 cup butter and 1 1/2 cups sugar

very thoroughly, add 4 beaten egg yolks, beat mixture well, adding 1/2 cup milk and the cup of flour. After beating thoroughly add melted chocolate. Now put in rest of flour. Beat again. Add nuts, stirring well, and then fold in the stiff-beaten egg whites. Bake in a flat loaf in SLOW oven.

Frosting: 2 cups granulated sugar boiled in 1/2 cup water till it will harden in cold water. Pour syrup over stiff-beaten whites of 2 eggs. Add 2 squares of Baker's chocolate (melted) and a little vanilla. Beat till of right consistency to spread.

Prune Pudding

Soak overnight and stew slowly until tender 2 pounds of prunes. When cold, put through the meat grinder (coarse). Beat 7 eggs, add 2 cups brown sugar, stir out all lumps; add 2 teaspoons cinnamon, 1/3 teaspoon allspice, 1/3 teaspoon cloves, and 1 teaspoonful salt; then add 1 cup molasses and 4 cups flour, adding 1 cup of prune juice as needed. Stir until smooth. Add 3 cups bread crumbs and balance of juice; beat well and add prunes and lastly 3 cups minced suet. Stir all well and put into greased can; steam 3 hours.

Lamb Pot Roast with Carrots

Take a large roast of lamb (the neck may be used) wipe dry with clean rag. Insert a small slice of garlic in gashes cut in meat (these need to be removed after cooking). Place in roasting pan, dust with flour, salt and pepper and place a large slice of fat bacon over the top. When meat is nearly done, tomatoes and carrots may be added to the juice in the roasting pan.

Chicken Pot Pie

Cut up chicken in large pieces after bird has been cooked so that the meat readily separates from the bones (boiling). Dice potatoes and add to chicken broth, which has been thickened with flour; cut celery fine and place all in earthenware pot pie dishes and season. Cover with ordinary rich pie crust and bake until brown. Parsley also may be cut fine and added if desired.

WASHINGTON

Apple Pie

Sift together 1 1/2 cupfuls pastry flour, 1/2 teaspoonful salt, and 1/2 teaspoonful baking powder; add 1/3 cupful shortening and chop lightly till well blended. Moisten to a dough with ice water, adding it gradually and cutting it in with a knife. Divide in halves and place half on a floured board; roll out deftly and line a pie pan. Thoroughly mix 1 tablespoonful flour with 3 tablespoonfuls sugar and sprinkle evenly over the crust. Fill the pan with 5 to 6 apples cut in eighths. Mix 3 tablespoonfuls sugar with 1/4 teaspoonful cinnamon and sprinkle over all. Dot with 1 tablespoonful of butter cut in bits; add 1 tablespoonful of water. Wet the edges of the lower crust and cover with the top crust in which gashes have been cut. Press the edges down firmly, sprinkle with cold water, and bake 40 minutes at 450 degrees.

Salmon Supreme

Measure 4 cupfuls freshly cooked or canned salmon, reserving the liquor. Remove the skin and bones and chop fine. Add 4 tablespoonfuls melted butter or margarine, 1 1/2 teaspoonfuls salt, 1/8 teaspoonful pepper, 1 tablespoon minced parsley, and 3 tablespoonfuls chopped celery. Beat 4 eggs well, combine with 1/2 cupful cracker crumbs and add to the first mixture. Mix well, pack into a buttered mold, and steam 1 hour. Turn out on a hot platter, garnish with 2 cupfuls cooked peas heated and seasoned to taste, and serve with the following sauce:

84

Scald 1 cupful milk. Combine 1/2 cupful salmon liquor and 1 table-spoonful cornstarch and add gradually to the milk, stirring constantly. Then add 1 tablespoonful butter, 1/2 teaspoonful salt, 1/8 teaspoonful pepper, and cook 3 minutes. Just before serving add 1 tablespoonful tomato catchup a little at a time.

Wild Duck

The wild ducks are bled and cleaned, but not plucked. The bird, feathers and all, is then rolled in a clean clay so that it is completely covered to a thickness of about 1/4 inch. Next a bed of hot coals is prepared and the bird is placed upon it and covered with a thick coat of green leaves or ferns. Since it is virtually impossible to burn the bird by this method, it may be left in its open-air oven until ready to be eaten. When the cooked bird is removed from the fire, the clay, which now holds all the feathers fast, is broken off, and the bird is ready to eat. The clay seals in all the juices. A better flavored or more tender bird is impossible by all other methods.

Meat Pancakes

To a cupful of cold meat add a few raisins chopped fine and season with salt, paprika, the pulp of a lemon, nutmeg, sugar, and 1 teaspoon of finely chopped pepper; add an egg and heat the mixture. Combine 3 eggs, a pint of milk, and enough flour to make a thin batter. After beating thoroughly, drop the batter in large spoonfuls on a hot and well-greased frying pan. As each cake browns on one side, place some of the meat mixture on it and fold the cake over the mixture. Then place the cakes in another pan containing a little meat stock and butter, and steam for 5 to 10 minutes.

WYOMING

Fish Chowder

Doc Rickert, who lives in Little Boulder Basin, and who blazed trails all over western Wyoming when he was a pioneer in the Forest Service, is an authority when it comes to Fish Chowder cooked in a Dutch oven. According to his instructions, you first dig a hole about 2 1/2 feet deep and 30 inches across. Build a timber fire in it. Let this burn for 2 hours, replenishing it with fuel now and then.

In the meantime, put bacon in a Dutch oven, then a layer of trout. If the fish are large cut them up and split them in two. Next spread a layer of raw Irish potato cubed, and then a layer of sliced onion. On top of that place another layer of fish and repeat the layers in order until the vessel is filled. Add a small slice of salt pork. Cover the whole with water and place over an open fire. Bring to a boil, then set off. As soon as the fire in the hole has become a mass of coals, shovel the coal out, except a layer of about 3 inches. Then add a cup of cold water to the chowder to check a sudden boil, place the lid on the Dutch oven, and lower the oven upon the bed of coals. Then bank the remaining coals on top and all around the oven. Cover with dirt and tramp down firmly. At the end of 24 hours, open the hole with care to prevent the ashes from getting into the oven. Lift up the lid and a perfect concoction will be found.

Fried Steak

Have the grease in the skillet smoking hot. This is vital. The meat must be quickly seared to retain its juices. Turn over quickly to seal the other side. This will also prevent the steak from absorbing grease. To properly fry steak is a real accomplishment. Do not salt steak before frying. Salt shrinks meat fibers and toughens it. Immediately after the steak is seared on both sides pour off most of the grease, it having served its purpose, which is to seal in the juices. Turn steak frequently to prevent it from becoming too crisp.

Mulligan

Another roundup dish, a sort of glorified "mulligan," is often prepared by the skillful Dutch oven cook. Have the desired quantity of meat cut in 2-inch chunks. In the words of the roundup cook, put "plenty grease," cooking oil, or other shortening into the hot Dutch oven, roll meat in flour to which a small amount of salt and pepper has been added, and brown quickly. Add water to cover. Cook until meat is tender, 1 to 2 hours. The Dutch oven is ideal for cooking meat in camp, as being air tight, it acts as a pressure cooker. When the meat is tender, add onions, thinly sliced or chopped, and potatoes, peeled and quartered. Cook until vegetables are done. For the "tenderfoot" it will be necessary to watch the amount of fire used and to keep sufficient water around the meat for the appetizing gravy that characterizes this dish.

A variation of the mulligan can be prepared by dicing meat and vegetables and cooking with water and seasonings. The gravy is thickened when the meat and vegetables are done by adding a little flour mixed to a paste with cold water. The result is a wet hash, which poured over sourdough biscuits, is not to be discounted for an evening meal in the open.

Special Sauce for Boiled Fish

Place 2 tablespoonfuls of butter and same amount of flour into a hot pan and mix to a smooth paste over the fire. Then pour over this paste a pint of hot water (prefer using the water the fish were boiled in) and stir well. Bring to a boil and season to suit. A few drops of lemon juice added improve the flavor.

Mustard Sauce for Boiled Fish

This is a good sauce for the coarser species of fish. Melt a quantity of butter equal in size to a large egg in hot pan over the fire; stir in a tablespoonful of flour and 1/2 teaspoonful of ground mustard. Season to suit. Bring to boil, and it is ready to use.

Photo Credits

All photos are from the WPA collection, Merrill G. Burlingame Special Collections in the Renne Library at Montana State University, Bozeman.

Index

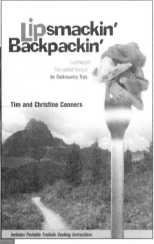

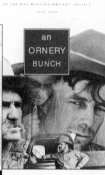